HOLY SPIRIT PRAYERS

Becoming One with the Father

by Michael Kirwin

God speaks a message through Scripture.

The Spirit within you responds in prayer.

Cover: 99Designs (Vista) by Designer Ryanurz

If you enjoyed these prayers and think others might benefit from them, please consider reviewing the book on Amazon. Author's mailing address is: PO Box 7. Clifford, PA 18413-007. Author's email: symeon.7.theologian@gmail.com

ISBN: 978-1-959608-98-1

PREFACE

I f the world were to judge my life as it stands today, it would most certainly label me a failure. Yes, you read that right. I have lost my dreams, my job, my health, my retirement savings, my friends, and even my home.

When I first became a pastor, I envisioned myself as another Billy Graham, ministering and preaching to millions. Young people dream big! This vision fueled my passion for crafting sermons each Sunday. I spent hours each week reading, reflecting and writing out my sermons. I wanted people to draw as close as possible to the voice of Jesus through the word. I wanted to set souls on fire with the Spirit. Every week I tried to minister to the community by visiting the sick, leading bible study groups, an inspirational book club, counseling and so on. It was exhausting but I loved being a pastor. My 46 years of ministry was a wonderful journey surrounded by truly remarkable, devoted, struggling and loving Christians. It was both a privilege and an honor to serve.

Yet, dreams are not always pleasant, nor do they always end as we hope. Now, in my older years, I look back at the fruits of my labor. I served eight different church communities. Of these, two dwindled in membership and transitioned to mission churches without a resident pastor. Five of these communities no longer exist—one church has been demolished to make way for a parking lot, three stand abandoned as worthless real estate, and one has become a bocce ball court. Only one community remains as an independent church, but its membership is dwindling. So much for the dream of a crowded stadium packed with Christians eager to hear the Word through my voice!

Soon after my ordination, I took on a second ministry and built up a promising radio ministry. It had great potential until my bishop decided it would be better served under another's leadership. He ordered me to resign and promised that the work would continue with his blessing and our denomination's financial support. The bishop lied! He had no desire to spread the Good News of Jesus. No one was ever assigned to continue the radio ministry. Within a year, every recorded sermon and all the equipment purchased for the ministry was destroyed. I was bewildered, deeply hurt, and disillusioned. Why would the bishop oppose the spread of God's Word? I felt like I was living inside a nightmare. I contemplated leaving ministry completely. Satan works hardest within the Church, raising up wolves in sheep's clothing to act as a cancer to destroy the body of Christ on earth. Strike the shepherd and the sheep will scatter. The Spirit spoke to me. I turned my frustration, anger, confusion and disillusionment over to Jesus and recommitted myself to serving the Lord.

I am now seventy-four and retired, living with Parkinson's disease. The symptoms seemed to appear overnight—my hand began to tremble; my speech was sometimes garbled and twice I lost my way while driving and couldn't figure out where I was or where I was going! Over the previous two years, I made impulsive, unwise decisions that wiped out 96 percent of my retirement savings. I could no longer afford the mortgage on a family home I had refinanced. Though I could still deliver Sunday sermons—thanks to typing out every word in advance—I struggled with simple, everyday conversations. I felt embarrassed, humiliated, and overwhelmed. I abruptly resigned from my pastorate. The thought of standing in a reception line, trying to say good-bye to friends when my speech was faltering, was too much to bear. I explained my health issues in a letter to the parish community and quietly stepped away.

My sudden departure, with no farewell reception, angered some people. I wonder now if that's why so many of the people I thought friends ignore my text messages.

At first, I wallowed in self-pity. I mourned the loss of my health, my dreams, my work, my retirement savings, my home, and my friendships. Loss was not new to me. I lost my childhood to a perpetually angry, alcoholic father. I now felt my earlier experience of loss compounded. For a few months, I let misery consume me. I couldn't imagine eventually spending the last two years of my life in a nursing home like my mother had who died of Parkinson's. I recall stepping out of the room so the nurses-aids could change her diapers and her screaming out from terrifying hallucinations. I needed a way out. Sorry to say, I actually went online to search out "Compassionate Friends" that might assist with my death.

But then, I began to reflect on my experience. Doesn't everyone, including Jesus, experience loss? You, dear reader, have faced loss. Your grief may be far more intense than mine. I have never buried a child or a spouse. I have never walked thousands of miles toward an uncertain future with no welcoming arms at the journey's end. My loss pales in comparison to that of so many others. As Christians, we cannot let loss or fear define us. Jesus must define us. Our lives should make no sense to the world except for the presence of Jesus. I needed to stop seeing myself as a victim.

I invite you to join me. Let's stop feeling sorry for ourselves. We are not victims. We have Jesus! Stand with me on the solid rock that is Christ, and together, let us lift our voices to God in praise and gratitude. Every event in our lives is a gift meant to draw us into communion with the Creator and with one another. God's blessings are more numerous than the raindrops in a summer storm! God is good. Jesus, the

Only Son of God, has chosen you to know His name. You have been chosen to receive His Holy Spirit. You have been called out of this world to join God in His eternal Kingdom. This world is not your home; it is not my home.

God did not place me on this earth to achieve success as the world defines it. My role was simply to plant seeds. Others will come to water them and watch them grow. If not, and it is God's will, those seeds will rot as if never spoken. Everything is a mist. God did not call you or me to worldly success. He called us to know Him, love Him, and serve Him. If your hands are empty, rejoice! Lift them up in prayer. The Holy Spirit inspired me to write this book as a gift to you. Open your heart now. God is speaking to you. Listen!

Michael Kirwin

TABLE OF CONTENTS

INTRODUCTION

The Bible is our ultimate user's manual for life. Just as a car's manual tells you how to maintain it, the Bible provides the divine guidance we need to navigate our lives. Consider the story of a young mechanic-in-training I visited at a hospital. He was recovering from surgery after a truck tire exploded while he was inflating it, embedding rubber in his skull. He hadn't checked the manual for the correct tire pressure. In much the same way, when we neglect the Bible, we risk harm in our lives.

If you seek to live a joyful, peaceful, and fulfilling life, becoming the best version of yourself, turn to the User's Manual for Human Life, authored by God over the span of a thousand years. As Jesus reminds us, "Man shall not live on bread alone, but on every word that comes from the mouth of God" (Matthew 4:4).

The Bible answers our deepest questions. Reflect on the night Jesus spent in the Garden of Gethsemane before His arrest. Satan tempted Him, offering a way out of the suffering that awaited Him. This moment, known as the Great Temptation, involved three questions that touched on the values of a world estranged from God: pleasure, wealth, and power. Where did Jesus find His answers? He turned to Scripture. Each of His three responses began with the words

"It is written" (Matthew 4:4, 7, 10). In the same way, all our questions can be answered by turning to the Word of God—our User's Manual for Human Life.

How to read the bible. Reading the Bible is an essential part of every Christian's faith journey. As we move through life, we all face questions and challenges.

Read it on your own. The Holy Spirit dwells within you and will illuminate the Scriptures as you read. "The Spirit of God lives in you" (Romans 8:9).

Listen to pastors. Just as we trust specialists for our medical needs, we should also turn to those who have devoted their lives to understanding God's Word. Pastors and Bible scholars, who may focus on different parts of Scripture, offer valuable insights. Be humble before the Lord, recognizing that others may have deeper knowledge. "We have different gifts, according to the grace given to each of us. If your gift is prophesying, then prophesy in accordance with your faith; if it is serving, then serve; if it is teaching, then teach" (Romans 12:6-7).

Join bible study groups. These groups can be incredibly enriching. The Holy Spirit bestows various gifts upon people for the building up of the Church—some may have a gift for hearing the Spirit in Scripture, others in teaching or interpretation. Sharing the Word in a group allows these diverse gifts to open up the meaning and application of Bible passages in powerful ways (see 1 Corinthians 12:4-31).

Whether alone or with others, our goal in reading Scripture is to listen for God's voice, reflect on what we hear, and respond in prayer. "All Scripture is God-breathed and is useful for teaching, rebuking, correcting and training in righteousness, so that the servant of God may be thoroughly equipped for every good work" (2 Timothy 3:16-17).

Christian literature. Not all of us are Bible scholars, and some may not have access to study groups or church fellowship. Sometimes, reading Scripture alone can be confusing. This is where Christian literature, Bible tracts, YouTube videos, and series like The Chosen can support our spiritual growth. My own inspiration to write this book came from reading *Grace for Purpose* by Hosiah Hope, along with spending time with their YouTube Scriptural Meditations.

Choosing a Bible. There are many Bible translations available, each offering different nuances. Throughout this book, I will primarily quote from the New International Version, a popular choice among many evangelical communities.

Jesus said, "And I will ask the Father, and he will give you another advocate to help you and be with you forever—the Spirit of truth. The world cannot accept him, because it neither sees him nor knows him. But you know him, for he lives with you and will be in you" (John 14:16-18).

This book assumes that you have received the Holy Spirit and seek communion with the Father. Jesus tells us that He is one with the Father, and through Him, we become one with God through the Spirit. This communion—becoming one with God—is the ultimate purpose of our existence.

God does speak to people of all time through scripture, but it is also true that God speaks through scripture to each of us in our own individual and unique lives. This book attempts to illuminate this truth. The first part of each section is titled "God is Speaking. Listen!" where a biblical teaching is presented. This is followed by an individual prayer response titled "My Prayer." As you read, it may be helpful to remember that the Greek word for "spirit" means "breath." It may help to imagine your breath as the Spirit, who is the source of all life (Romans 8:2). Praying in the Spirit draws you closer to the origin of all life.

The Spirit is already within you! The challenge in prayer is simply to become aware of God's presence. Open the door of your heart. Invite the Spirit in. Read slowly and with intention.

"In the same way, the Spirit helps us in our weakness. We do not know what we ought to pray for, but the Spirit himself intercedes for us through wordless groans. And he who searches our hearts knows the mind of the Spirit, because the Spirit intercedes for God's people in accordance with the will of God."

Romans 8:26-27

CHAPTER 1

YOU ARE NOT ALONE

God is speaking to you. Listen!

Why have you felt so alone? Abandoned? Forgotten? Rejected? Was it the pain you endured when your friend betrayed you, when your sister quarreled with you over the will, when your spouse fell out of love, when your children grew up and never thought to call, or when your employer overlooked you for a bonus? Was it because your name wasn't included with the others? Was it the illness that made you think I was not there? Was it the grief, the emptiness, the despair when death carved a hole in your heart?

Consider the life of Moses for insight into your experience. Moses knew the depths of abandonment. He grew up with Ramesses II, the boy who would become Pharaoh. They were best friends, like family—brothers. But all this was forgotten when Ramesses learned that Moses was a child of Israel. One moment they were brothers, and the next, Moses was nothing to him. Moses was never given a chance to plead his case, explain himself, ask for mercy, or even thank Ramesses for their friendship. Instead, he was sentenced to death and fled into the wilderness. Moses knew he was no longer a person to Pharaoh and so had no voice with which to speak. He was cast aside without a second thought, regarded as nothing more than garbage in Pharaoh's mind. Imagine the trauma of seeing all your memories of family and friendship evaporate in one moment. These boys had played together by the Nile, laughed through the palace, and marveled at the creatures they found. Yet, in an instant, the entire relationship was swept away like ashes in the wind. Moses was a Jew, and to Pharaoh, that meant he did not count. Moses was alone. His imagined past no longer existed, and his adoptive family was no more. Unsure of who he was, Moses fled into the desert.

Many of you have had a similar experience. Take Catherine (a fictitious name), for example. She was happily married for forty-four years, with three wonderful children and four grandchildren. Then one day, her husband walked in and said, "I don't love you anymore. I never loved you!" Her first instinct was to dig out the family photo albums. She showed him photos from years of birthday parties, vacations, and family meals. "Look! Isn't this you in the photo laughing? How can you say you were never happy? It just isn't true." Her world began to spin. The walls of the room where she sat didn't seem straight. The floor wasn't level. She had to sit down. Later that afternoon, he moved his things into his girlfriend's apartment.

But I, the God of Israel, had a plan for Moses and for Catherine. You think it was fortune or luck that led Moses to the land of Midian, where he met his wife? It was not her adult children, friends, or gifted therapists that led Catherine through her mental breakdown to a new life. It was Me. I never left her side. I have a plan for you, too. Get up and go back to Egypt.

Recall Jeremiah's story. They called him "the weeping proph-et." The people I had blessed and protected forgot Me and turned to other gods. I chose Jeremiah to deliver My word to the people. He felt totally inadequate for the job.

"I can't speak," he told Me.

"Don't worry, Jeremiah, I will give you the words."

Jeremiah relented but not without his doubts. The words I put in his mouth were harsh—destruction and exile awaited the people if they did not change their ways. Yet, the people would not listen. Everyone turned on Jeremiah. His fellow priests plotted against him, the people hated him, and the rulers did not trust him. Jeremiah suffered. He was scorned and humiliated, locked in a stockade, mocked by passersby, beaten, and thrown into a cistern to starve. Jeremiah felt alone. Or so he thought.

He had Me. I was there. Always. When Jeremiah complained and asked for help, I told him the truth: "Expect things to only get worse!" And they did get worse.

But though Jeremiah complained, he remained faithful. He outlived five kings and passed into old age. His life was not easy. Every single day, Jeremiah needed to remind himself that I was with him. And so do you.

The Samaritan woman Jesus met at the well also experienced the worst in people. My Son, Jesus, met her at the hottest hour of the day when everyone with an ounce of sense was shut up inside trying to escape the heat. She chose that time to get water because she knew no one else would be at the well. Much better to endure the heat than the scorns, derision, and curses of her neighbors. Outcast. Dirty whore. She was not only a member of the "wrong" religion, nationality, and gender, but she had slept with seven different men!

Then Jesus appeared before her. This prophet, My Son, knew everything about her and loved her anyway. He saw her courage. She never gave up and was determined to find love. But she was alone. Terribly alone. Until Jesus spoke to her. He told her He was the "living water."

"I love you just as you are. I see into your heart. In many ways, it is your weakness where I find your greatest strength. I hear your pleas for reassurance, escape, a friend. The path was set for your life before you could speak. Part of your journey is suffering. You are no longer a child, so let Me speak the truth: Things may never get better."

Not even Jesus escaped moments of profound abandonment. Jesus prayed in the Garden of Gethsemane. "My Father, if it is possible, may this cup be taken from me. Yet not as I will, but as you will" (Matthew 26:39). The cup did not pass. The darkness grew more powerful. Neither Moses, nor Jeremiah, nor the woman with forty-four years of marriage, nor the Samaritan woman, nor Jesus were ever alone. You are not alone either.

The very last words I spoke to you through the mouth of Jesus before He ascended to heaven were very important: "And surely I am with you always, to the very end of the age" (Matthew 28:20). "Always" means right now. When you feel alone, you must remind yourself that statement is a lie. You are not alone. I have spoken. You are never alone.

My words in Scripture are meant for your ears. My words are meant to lift up your heart from darkness. My words are truth. The voice of darkness will never tire in its battle for your soul. It lies. No one will take you from Me. I am at your side.

The psalmist cried out to Me when he felt abandoned: "Do not turn me over to the desire of my foes, for false witnesses rise up against me, spouting malicious accusations. I remain confident of this: I will see the goodness of the LORD in the land of the living. Wait for the LORD; be strong and take heart and wait for the LORD" (Psalm 27:12-14). Wait for Me, My child. You will see green pastures once again.

"So do not fear, for I am with you; do not be dismayed, for I am your God. I will strengthen you and help you; I will uphold you with my righteous right hand" (Isaiah 41:10). "For I am the LORD your God who takes hold of your right hand and says to you, Do not fear; I will help you" (Isaiah 41:13).

"Do not let your hearts be troubled. You believe in God; believe also in me."

John 14:1

"I will not leave you orphans; I will come to you."

John 14:18

My Prayer

Jesus, You are my friend. You know how alone I feel right now. Forsaken. Diminished. Depleted. Empty. Overwhelmed. Abandoned. I feel like Elijah in the desert, his face against the sand, his eyes closed, his mind unable to muster the strength to say out loud some of his burning questions: "I can't go on. What is real? What is good? Who cares about me?"

But here You are, Jesus. You reach down into the dark waters and lift me up. I feel Your arms holding me to Yourself. The warmth of Your chest against my own, the soft touch of Your beard, the sweetness of Your breath.

"Shh" slips from Your lips. "Shh." No words are necessary. You rock me back and forth like an infant.

"To you, LORD, I call; you are my Rock, do not turn a deaf ear to me. For if you remain silent, I will be like those who go down to the pit. Hear my cry for mercy as I call to you for help, as I lift up my hands toward your Most Holy Place" (Psalm 28:1-2).

But You are not far off, needing to be summoned, for You, Lord, are always here at my side; indeed, Your Spirit is within my heart. I only need say Your name, Jesus, and You are there.

"Praise be to the LORD, for he has heard my cry for mercy. The LORD is my strength and my shield; my heart trusts in him, and he helps me. My heart leaps for joy, and with my song I praise him" (Psalm 28:6-7).

"Be strong and courageous, and do the work. Do not be afraid or discouraged, for the LORD God, my God, is with you. He will not fail you or forsake you..." (1 Chronicles 28:20). I hear You, Lord. Do the work? Yes, life is to be lived, opportunities taken, prayers offered, and hearts healed. Turn my attention outside myself to Your mission and help me stop feeling this wretched self-pity. Do the work. I remember what You said to the prophet Elijah who

gave up and collapsed in the desert: "Get up and eat." (1 Kings 19:5)

I know I am repeating myself, Lord, but Your words to Joshua really speak to what I am going through right now: "As I was with Moses, so I will be with you; I will never leave you nor forsake you. Be strong and courageous" (Joshua 1:5b, 6a). "Be strong and courageous. Do not be afraid; do not be discouraged, for the LORD your God will be with you wherever you go" (Joshua 1:9). You know how critically important these words are because constantly throughout Scripture, You speak this same powerful word to the abandoned: "You are not alone." And to assure that each person can be restored to peace, You gift us Your Spirit to make it happen: "The Spirit of truth. The world cannot accept him, because it neither sees him nor knows him. But you know him, for he lives with you and will be in you. I will not leave you as orphans; I will come to you" (John 14:17-18).

You know, Lord, how hard I try to keep Your commandments and live out my love for others. Fulfill Your promise merciful Jesus, and reveal Yourself to me. Help me to feel Your presence and experience Your Holy Spirit in my life. Save me from depression and despair. Remind me over and over again that I am not alone, and help me to believe it and feel it. I am not alone. Jesus, speak "peace" to me. "Peace I leave with you; my peace I give you" (John 14:27).

I renounce all my fear and trouble. I will not be afraid. I will not hide away or put my face to the ground, Jesus. Come, Holy Spirit. Peace. I say it again, peace. And again, peace.

I feel something—a warmth, perhaps a light, a presence—surround my head and begin to make its way down through my head, my neck, my shoulders, my chest and buttocks, my thighs, legs, and feet. Peace. Comfort. Jesus, Your Spirit is resting upon me. As the Father loved You, Jesus, You love me. It was not I who chose You, Jesus. You chose me! You appointed this life for me. What I do and say will bear fruit according to Your will. It is Your plan, Lord. Help me bloom where I am planted, here in this life at this moment in time (see John 14).

I must stop grieving the past and fearing the future. I declare an end to the rule of fear over my life. "Be strong and courageous. Do not be afraid or terrified...for the LORD your God goes with you; he will never leave you or forsake you" (Deuteronomy 31:6). "Trust in the LORD with all your heart and lean not on your own understanding; in all your ways submit to him, and he will make your paths straight" (Proverbs 3:5-6).

I hear Your voice, Father. "Can a mother forget the baby at her breast and have no compassion on the child she has borne? Though she may forget, I will not forget you! See, I have engraved you on the palms of my hands; your walls are ever before me" (Isaiah 49:15-16).

Praise and glory to You, Jesus, my friend. You save me from myself. You have rescued me. **Spoken in the Spirit through Jesus, the Son, to the Father. Amen.**

CHAPTER 2

YOU ARE THE LIGHT

God is speaking to you. Listen!

"And God said, 'Let there be light,' and there was light. God saw that the light was good and he separated the light from the darkness" (Genesis 1: 3-4). I made the dry earth and the oceans of the world and saw how "good" it was (v. 10). I made the vegetation that covers the earth and saw how good it was (v.12). Your eyes open to a good world. And you, My child, are the center of that goodness. "You are the light of the world. A town built on a hill cannot be hidden" (Matthew 5:14). It is not just the day and the night, the mountains and the oceans, the plants and animals that are good. Humankind is good (Genesis 1:31). You, as an individual person, are good. I made you in My image, so how could you think otherwise? "Don't you know that you yourselves are God's temple and that God's Spirit dwells in your midst?" (1 Corinthians 3:16).

From the first moment you open your eyes in the morning, I want you to be filled with a sense of wonder at the goodness that surrounds you and the goodness you are. Gratitude. Gratitude is the beginning of our journey together. "Give thanks in all circumstances; for this is God's will for you in Christ Jesus" (1 Thessalonians 5:18).

Gratitude lifts your mind and heart. It reaches out and is our first touch every morning. Let the good you experience move you to words of praise. Let the goodness you feel cast away the darkness of the night. Everything you experience in creation should remind you that I AM. It is God, your Father, who speaks. Listen to My voice. Everything reflects My goodness. You were made to see this truth. You were made to speak this truth. You are the light.

Gratitude. Praise. Glory. "For the Spirit God gave us does not make us timid, but gives us power, love, and self-discipline" (2 Timothy 1:7). Take control of your thoughts and choose to think about good things. "Whatever is true, whatever is noble, whatever is right, whatever is pure, whatever is lovely, whatever is admirable—if anything is excellent or praiseworthy—think about such things. Whatever you have learned or received or heard from Me, or seen in Me—put it into practice. And the God of peace will be with you" (Philippians 4:8-9).

Choose to see the good. Choose to be positive. Choose to walk in the light. "Your eye is the lamp of your body. When your eyes are healthy, your whole body also is full of light. But when they are unhealthy, your body also is full of darkness" (Luke 11:34). If your eye is searching for evil, it will find it. If your eye searches for what is good and honorable, it will find it. Set your mind on searching each person for the good within them. Name the good. Be a light to your neighbor, and you will become a light unto yourself.

"For you were once darkness, but now you are light in the Lord. Live as children of light (for the fruit of the light consists in all goodness,

> *righteousness, and truth) and find out what*
> *pleases the Lord."*
>
> Ephesians 5:8-10

> *"Set your minds on things above, not on earthly*
> *things."*
>
> Colossians 3:2

> *"Do not let any unwholesome talk come out*
> *of your mouths, but only what is helpful for*
> *building others up according to their needs,*
> *that it may benefit those who listen. And do not*
> *grieve the Holy Spirit of God, with whom you*
> *were sealed for the day of redemption. Get rid*
> *of all bitterness, rage, and anger, brawling and*
> *slander, along with every form of malice. Be kind*
> *and compassionate to one another, forgiving each*
> *other, just as in Christ God forgave you."*
>
> Ephesians 4:29-32

"Do not conform to the pattern of this world, but be transformed by the renewing of your mind. Then you will be able to test and approve what God's will is—His good, pleasing, and perfect will" (Romans 12:2). Choose to be positive. Choose to be light!

"The light shines in the darkness, and the darkness has not overcome it" (John 1:5). I know ugliness exists in this world, including greed, murder, lust, selfishness, death, and idolatry. I know the struggle to exist, to survive, and to thrive when the darkness continues its unrelenting impulse to take the universe back into the original abyss. But it is I who have written this story, and the light cannot be vanquished. Darkness cannot overcome the light. I need you, as disciples of My Son, Jesus, to be intent and unrelenting in your quest to center your mind on the good around you. I need you to speak of the good to affirm it and to nurture it.

St. Paul quotes Me, and then he reminds you of something very important about the darkness you may experience. The light within you is the Holy Spirit. The Spirit will give you the strength to walk in the steps of Jesus. The Spirit, who is the light, will help you persevere as children of the Way.

"For God, who said, 'Let light shine out of darkness,' made His light shine in our hearts to give us the light of the knowledge of God's glory displayed in the face of Christ. But we have this treasure in jars of clay to show that this all-surpassing power is from God and not from us. We are hard-pressed on every side, but not crushed; perplexed, but not in despair; persecuted, but not abandoned; struck down, but not destroyed. We always carry around in our body the death of Jesus, so that the life of Jesus may also be revealed in our body. For we who are alive are always being given over to death for Jesus' sake, so that His life may also be revealed in our mortal body" (2 Corinthians 4:6-11).

"Darkness covers the earth and thick darkness is over the peoples" (Isaiah 60:2). You are called to build the kingdom of God in this foreign land. It is your witness to the teaching of Jesus that will give birth to light within others. "You are all children of the light and children of the day. We do not belong to the night or to the darkness" (1 Thessalonians 5:5).

My Prayer

Father, it was Jesus who invited me to use the word Abba when speaking to You. I understand it is the familiar term children who speak Arabic use for Father. It means Daddy! We are not just Creator and creature. We are parent and child. I am not just made by You, but I am part of You.

Abba, help me to see the light. Help me to be a light. Open my mind to the good that surrounds me. Let everything remind me of Your love and care: the room I sleep in, the blankets and pillow on my bed, the roof over my head, my access to indoor plumbing and clean water, the clothes I put on in the morning, a table to sit at, a stove and refrigerator. People who love and care for me: my mom and dad, sisters and brothers, grandparents, schoolmates, friends, neighbors, to name a few. Thank You. A safe place to call home, the sound of birds chirping, the first tree I see each day, the ability to see and hear and think. Thank You. I am awake. I am alive. All of this is because of You. You put me here. You chose this time and place and these people I love for me. Creator-God. Abba. Daddy. I praise You for Your name, "I AM."

Gratitude. You led me here, and I am in wonder and awe at Your goodness. Thank You. "Every good and perfect gift is from above, coming down from the Father of the heavenly lights, who does not change like shifting shadows" (James 1:17). "Give thanks to the LORD, for He is good; His love endures forever" (1 Chronicles 16:34). Thank You, Father, Abba. "Because of the LORD's great love, we are not consumed, for His compassions never fail. They are new each morning; great is Your faithfulness" (Lamentations 3:22-23).

I will not be anxious about anything, Father. Your Holy Spirit breathes within me; Your peace flows through me.

Father, this peace I experience surpasses my understanding. I just know the simple truth that with Jesus, my heart and my mind are shielded from darkness, and nothing can happen that is beyond Your love and care. I belong to You (Philippians 4). I stand in Your presence, Father, with thanksgiving; I make joyful noise to You with music and songs (Psalm 95:2).

The light of Your Spirit within me is a witness that You are truly the God of Israel, the One God. You and Jesus are one, and because of His Spirit, I am one with You, eternal and living God. "You are worthy, our Lord and God, to receive glory and honor and power, for You created all things, and by Your will they were created and have their being" (Revelation 4:11). "'Holy, holy, holy is the Lord God Almighty,' who was, and is, and is to come" (Revelation 4:8).

Spoken in the Spirit through Jesus, the Son, to the Father. Amen.

CHAPTER 3

THERE IS A REASON YOU ARE HERE

God is speaking to you. Listen!

I t is no accident that you are reading these words. You were led here, guided by My hand. Everything in your life is connected, part of a divine design. Before you took your first breath, I chose your parents, knew your name, and determined the color of your hair, your height, and the span of your life. "Before I formed you in the womb, I knew you, before you were born, I set you apart" (Jeremiah 1:5). Each day of your life has led to this moment, when you turn your thoughts to Me, Your Creator.

Now, this collection of atoms, molecules, and spirit that is you has found its voice and returned to the One who began it all. You are My creation, awakening to the truth of your origin and purpose. "No one can come to me unless the Father who sent me draws them, and I will raise them up on the last day" (John 6:44).

I have been your guide, your shepherd, and your protector, leading you to this very moment. "The Lord is my shepherd; I lack nothing. He makes me lie down in green pastures,

He leads me beside quiet waters, he refreshes my soul. He guides me along the right paths for his name's sake" (Psalm 23:1-3).

I planted within you a seed, a yearning for meaning that would awaken in its time. You have asked, "Why was I born? Why am I here? What is the purpose of my life? Surely, there must be more to life than working, eating, procreating, and seeking entertainment." I am your Maker, your Father, and it is in Me that you will find the answers you seek. I alone hold the pieces that will make you whole.

"In their hearts, humans plan their course, but the Lord establishes their steps" (Proverbs 16:9). I directed your steps to this moment. Just as the salmon returns from the cold depths of the ocean to its birthplace, so have you found your way back to the One who shaped you in the womb. Not everyone responds to My call. "For many are invited, but few are chosen" (Matthew 22:14). But you have answered.

"Here I am! I stand at the door and knock. If anyone hears my voice and opens the door, I will come in and eat with that person, and they with me" (Revelation 3:20). I have been knocking for quite some time now. I never force the door; it must be opened from within. I wait for an invitation. I have whispered many times: "Call to me and I will answer you and tell you great and unsearchable things you do not know" (Jeremiah 33:3).

My invitation is meant to soothe your spirit. My gentle words recognize how fragile you are. "Come to me, all you who are weary and burdened, and I will give you rest. Take my yoke upon you and learn from me, for I am gentle and humble in heart, and you will find rest for your souls" (Matthew 11:28-30).

There Is a Reason You Are Here

You were predestined for this moment. "For we know, brothers and sisters loved by God, that he has chosen you" (1 Thessalonians 1:4). Remember again, "No one can come to me unless the Father who sent me draws them" (John 6:44). I have drawn you to Myself. "For he chose us in him before the creation of the world to be holy and blameless in his sight. In love, he predestined us for adoption to sonship through Jesus Christ, in accordance with his pleasure and will—to the praise of His glorious grace, which he has freely given us in the one he loves" (Ephesians 1:4-6).

You now know My Name. Be confident in Me, for I am here with you. I have even rehearsed My response to your awakening. I say, "Yes." Yes, come to Me. I "will rejoice over you with singing" (Zephaniah 3:17). "I will bring you home" (Zephaniah 3:20).

My Prayer

Lord Jesus, "Here I am, I have come to do your will" (Hebrews 10:9). "I proclaim your saving acts in the great assembly; I do not seal my lips, Lord, as you know" (Psalm 40:9).

Lord, You said, "Whoever acknowledges me before others, I will also acknowledge before my Father in heaven" (Matthew 10:32). I speak your name, Jesus, and acknowledge your holy presence. Thank you for opening the eyes of my heart. I am grateful that you set me apart before I was born and called me by your grace (Galatians 1:15).

You stitched me together within the womb and breathed into me Your gift of life. Continue to pour forth Your Spirit upon me, Lord, and sustain me in my trials. Like a sculptor

29

before a block of marble, take Your hammer and chisel and make me into the person You first imagined. I know You are guiding my life, Jesus. I feel Your presence by my side. You chose the time and place of my first birth, and You choose me a second time to be born again in Your Spirit. My entire life, You have set each step before me, pushed me to swim across rivers that lead to You. Continue, Lord, to keep me on Your potter's wheel. Guide my decisions, choose the friendships I should cultivate and nurture, lead me to books that reveal Your truth, and author my words so that my life may witness to Your love.

Jesus, breathe into me Your Spirit and give me a compassionate heart, kindness, humility, meekness, and patience (Colossians 3:12). Let the dust and darkness that buries me inside this flesh and blood be hammered away. Though I am unworthy, open the gates of Your sanctuary and call me into Your holy presence. Forgive my lukewarm heart, my laziness, my caution in offering forgiveness. Help me to be trustworthy, reverent, steadfast, disciplined, and untiring in my endeavor to grow in the Spirit. Forgive my tendency to be easily discouraged. Redirect my negative thoughts to focus on the good and wonderful gifts that abound.

"And we know that in all things God works for the good of those who love him, who have been called according to his purpose. For those God foreknew he also predestined to be conformed to the image of his Son, that he might be the firstborn among many brothers and sisters" (Romans 8:28-29). Help me to accept and use the suffering I experience to grow as a follower of Jesus. My life has known failure and success, suffering and celebration, love and hate. Consecrate all the events of my past and help me to accept every experience as a gift. All things have worked to bring me here. I understand that by using every experience to

help me grow, I open myself to Your grace. I am the clay, Lord; You are the potter.

Father, You did not spare Your own Son from the horrors of life, so why should You spare me? (Romans 8:32). Lord, touch all the damaged parts of my mind and heart with healing. Remove resentment, bitterness, greed, and lust. Give me an understanding heart and pour Your wisdom into me. Let nothing separate me from You. "Who shall separate us from the love of Christ? Shall trouble or hardship or persecution or famine or nakedness or danger or sword?" (Romans 8:35). Will my sin separate me from You? Command, Jesus, that all things work together for good according to Your purpose. Let nothing separate me from You.

You, Jesus, see my past, present, and future. You stand outside and within time. You knew in advance of my every sin and every attempt to love. Before anything happens in my life, You already know how I might understand, reflect, and act. Shape my decisions that I might stay on the right path. Help me to conform and grow in Your image (Romans 8). You call me to live simply as Your follower and disciple. Help me to continue to live simply so that others may simply live. Open my mind to ways I might help my brothers and sisters with the gifts You have poured into my life. Let my life never bring shame to You, Lord. You invite me to become one with the Spirit of Jesus and one with His body on earth, the fellowship of believers. Thank You! It is through Jesus that I seek to become one with You, Father.

"For those God foreknew he also predestined to be conformed to the image of his Son" (Romans 8:29). "And those he predestined, he also called; those he called, he also justified; those he justified, he also glorified" (Romans 8:30).

Jesus, allow Your glory to shine into my heart and from my heart upon the world. Let the living waters of Your Spirit pour forth into the lives of others through everything I say and do. Kindle in me the fire of Your love. Look with mercy upon me as You looked upon the woman caught in adultery. Lord, You did not criticize or reprimand her. Your words were tender. You called her "woman," the same word You invoked for Your mother when You spoke from the cross. You therein made the Samaritan woman a member of Your family. "Woman," You said, "has no one condemned you? Neither do I condemn you!" Please do not condemn me, Jesus.

Jesus, look with mercy upon me. Wash me of my sins. Restore my confidence, my innocence, my self-worth. Continue to look upon me as both family and friend. You say, "I am making everything new" (Revelation 21:5). Make me new again, Jesus. Lift me up as You lifted the Samaritan woman from the prison of her isolation.

"In the time of my favor I heard you, and in the day of salvation I helped you. Now is the time of God's favor, now is the day of salvation" (2 Corinthians 6:2). Glory to You, Word of God, Lord Jesus Christ. "To Him who sits on the throne and to the Lamb be praise and honor and glory and power, for ever and ever!" (Revelation 5:13). Jesus is Lord!

Spoken in the Spirit through Jesus, the Son, to the Father. Amen.

CHAPTER 4

WHEN YOU REACH ROCK BOTTOM

God is speaking to you. Listen!

Are you there yet? Rock bottom. Alcoholics Anonymous coined this term to describe that point in addiction when the choice between life and death becomes starkly real—when there is no more time for fooling around. The chances to recover have run out. Usually, rock bottom finds the person stripped of every possession, every sense of personal dignity, every loving relationship, and every means of employment. At rock bottom, the only "friends" left are other addicts. Marriages and family life have disintegrated, sources of financial support are exhausted, and relationships have been so thoroughly abused that no one wants you around. People have had enough of your manipulation and simply want you to go away.

But there is another kind of rock bottom that comes from suffering, and almost every single human being will experience it. This is where you, dear reader, enter the story. This rock bottom can come after years of dealing with physical suffering like cancer, arthritis, MS, muscular dystrophy, or chronic migraines. It can come after years of grappling with mental suffering, such as depression, grief, anxiety, PTSD, or psychosis.

Most often, however, this rock bottom comes from a spiritual crisis. Spiritual suffering arises when you realize that, despite the blessings in your life, there is an ache, an emptiness within your heart—a thorn in your side that no human being or material possession can remove. It is an emptiness that nothing in this world can fill.

Not everyone becomes conscious of this emptiness. It is possible to live on the surface of life without reflection, never asking the deeper questions of how or why. But waking up to this emptiness, recognizing your misery, is the first step toward finding the remedy. Material objects, human relationships, careers, popularity, and power—all fail here. This emptiness is a spiritual vacuum, not physical or psychological. Ironically, those with the most blessings are often the most miserable and unhappy.

The rock bottom awakening to spiritual emptiness can best be described with the word "enough." You feel like you've had enough and just don't see a way forward. You don't want to do this alone anymore. Despite doctors and pills, vacations and nights out, self-help gurus and yoga, empty sex, and all the distractions of life, nothing is enough.

Whether gluttonous or starved, you find your life isn't working. You feel a deep unhappiness despite your fortune and blessings. This emptiness is a black hole that, if you stare at it long enough, will drag you into despair. You realize that no amount of striving, no amount of searching, will ever resolve this void on your own. A sense of despair settles in as you become aware that all your efforts have been in vain; all your searching is empty.

All three forms of suffering—spiritual, physical, and mental—are part of a journey designed by Me, your Creator, to lead you home to Me. Having journeyed through your self-made life, you need to realize that you've gotten nowhere. Your life is a mist, ephemeral and without substance.

You struggled so hard to achieve, to procure, and to become someone, but in the end, you realize that life is devoid of meaning without God, without Me. It is at this juncture that you are invited to open the door to your heart and believe that I stand on the other side, waiting to greet you. Opening this door is like jumping blindly from a cliff, trusting that I will be waiting with open arms to catch you. Choose to jump, to trust, to believe.

If you jump, you will know that I exist. I Am. I created you. I am love, and if you have loved, then you have already found Me. Love will outlive the physical universe. It will endure beyond the grave. Love chose to bless you with life. Love promises to take you by the hand and lead you home. I designed you with one missing piece that can make you whole. I am that missing piece. I Am. I am love. Love alone gives your life meaning.

My Prayer

Father, You have blessed me in countless ways, and for most of my life, I took my gifts for granted. You knit me together in my mother's womb, chose my hair color and height, my IQ, my artistic abilities (or lack thereof), my sense of humor, and even my teeth and bone density. I am grateful that You placed me in an age where medicine and technology alleviate so much suffering and expand the human experience. I don't think I'd have liked living in times when they drilled holes in your skull.

I am thankful for the comforts of this era—my iPhone, the internet, sewage systems, and air travel. I'm glad I don't have to deal with the hardships of ages past, like dumping human waste into the streets. I'm truly thankful for this time in history. Rarely have I reflected on the vast landscape of blessings You have placed in my life.

You chose all the members of my family: grandparents, parents, siblings, spouse, friends, infatuations, life partners, lovers, children and grandchildren, employers and coworkers, teachers and faith leaders. I've learned from all these people and been especially blessed by some. It is impossible for me to list all the blessings or gifts You have poured into my life. Your blessings are more numerous than the grains of sand on the ocean's shores.

Yahweh, Father of all, I declare You to be the source of all blessings. You are the giver, the benefactor, the one who renews Your blessings with the rising of the sun every day.

It's amazing that I entered places of worship as a child, sang hymns, half-listened to religious teachers, and never really even thought of You—not truly, not in the sense that You were more than a storybook character. I didn't relate to You as a person, as someone with feelings, dreams, wishes, expectations, and needs.

I prayed the Our Father with everyone else, lifted up prayers, and even sang hymns to Your glory, but mostly, they were just empty words spoken from an empty heart into an empty universe. It is strange. I was living in a universe filled with Your gifts and rarely felt You there at my side, watching me. And yet, You have been right here all the time, waiting for me to notice, listening for one word of thanks—genuine thanks. I was not grateful. Not really. Not to any emotional level. How could I be? I was living on the surface of life, and You, Lord, were not real.

But being here now, I think I've passed through that place— the rock bottom where nothing was enough. Lord, no one filled that hole, that emptiness, that vacuum within my life. I had so much, and yet, I was truly miserable. I had everything, and I see now that it all counted for nothing without You, Lord. I'm just now beginning to see You clear- ly. I believe that You came to earth in Jesus, fully human like me, but more! Emmanuel. You are God with us. You are real and alive.

Come, Lord Jesus, touch my eyes and heal my blindness. Touch my ears and let me truly hear Your voice. Let Your Word thunder through my mind and shake me from my complacency.

Open the spring of living water, Jesus, and let Your Holy Spirit rush forth, carrying away all within me that is not born of You. Forgive me for my apathy. Wash clean all the sin born of my callous treatment of others—my pride and arrogance, my superiority, my jealousy and greed. Burn away the lust that has plagued my mind and stained my soul. Be merciful to me for ignoring the cries of the hungry, homeless, disenfranchised, powerless, and those who suffer from systems of injustice. I have not lived simply so others may simply live.

I have been indifferent to the poor and at times blamed them for their want. I have judged people mercilessly and condemned Your church in my cruel disdain for Your peo- ple and Your ministers. I have singularly focused on what was wrong, evil, and hypocritical in others and completely overlooked the good that was always there.

I begin my spiritual journey through the pages of this prayer book with contrition, for I recognize that I am a sinner. I am a sinner not only in what I have done but also in all that I have failed to do or become. I have missed the mark, fallen short of Your call. I need You, Jesus. I need Your forgiveness. I need Your gift of faith. I need Your Holy Spirit. I need Your light and Your Word. Help me, Jesus. You are my Lord and my God. I am unworthy. Please be merciful to me, a sinner.

Spoken in the Spirit through Jesus, the Son, to the Father. Amen.

CHAPTER 5

GOD, IS IT YOU?

God is speaking to you. Listen!

"Then you will call on me and come and pray to me, and I will listen to you. You will seek me and find me when you seek me with all your heart."

Jeremiah 29:12-13

Yes, it is Me. "For since the creation of the world, God's invisible qualities—his eternal power and divine nature—have been clearly seen, being understood from what has been made, so that people are without excuse. For although they knew God, they neither glorified him as God nor gave thanks to him, but their thinking became futile and their foolish hearts were darkened" (Romans 1:20-21).

Learn from the story of Jesus' temptation in Gethsemane. The prince of this world promised Jesus riches, glory, and power if He would only turn from Me, the Father. Look around you and see the wealth of those who reject Me and My Son. See how blessed in this life are those who deny Me. The prince of this world promises stones will become bread to feed you, angels to protect you from physical harm, and power and glory if you but serve him. Others have accepted the same invitation made to Jesus by Satan and stand rewarded.

"Why do the wicked live on, growing old and increasing in power? They see their children established around them, their offspring before their eyes. Their homes are safe and free from fear; the rod of God is not on them. . . . They send forth their children as a flock; their little ones dance about. . . . They spend their years in prosperity and go down to the grave in peace."

Job 21:7-9, 11, 13

The righteous do not serve the prince of this world and are sometimes denied its most wondrous fruits. Yes, all are blessed with life, and indeed I send down rain on the fields of the just and the unjust. But to those who serve the Evil One, as well as all those who live without Me, I promise a wake-up call, a thorn in their side, an emptiness that cries out for an answer. It is only a delusion that this world and its riches can bring fulfillment, enlightenment, or spiritual peace.

C. S. Lewis said, "In religion, as in war and everything else, comfort is the one thing you cannot get by looking for it. If you look for truth, you may find comfort in the end: if you look for comfort, you will not get either comfort or truth, only soft soap and wishful thinking to begin with and, in the end, despair."[1] I made you with one missing piece. You are not whole, so you cannot be completely happy or satisfied in

---

1   C. S. Lewis, *Mere Christianity*

this world. You may search through all the wondrous works of My hand, experience the world's pleasures and treasures, and try out people and power to examine their size and fit. You will find nothing and no one to fill the emptiness I planted within your heart. Your quest is futile as long as your search is limited to this world. This world does not contain what you need.

Reach out to Me, the Creator. I am the peace you seek, and I do not bring it as the world delivers. You were made for My pleasure. You were made to know, love, and serve Me—not yourself.

People can spend their whole lives on the surface of living without ever opening the door of their hearts to Me, their Creator. My knocks and My pleas for recognition are ignored. Some people find Me easily because the abundance of gifts I shower into their lives wakes them to the fact that there is a Giver! Some people find Me because My fingerprints are on every created thing, and their wonder at what I made shouts out the fact that there is a higher power.

Some, however, cannot hear My whispers, so I blast the megaphone of suffering. It brings them to rock bottom, where illusions are stripped away. No more self-delusion or lies. All the voices that filled their minds are silent here. They face annihilation or the possibility that I am real. It is the absence of blessings at rock bottom that forces one to acknowledge that blessings existed. "I am near to the brokenhearted" (Psalm 34:18).

Only when the blessings disappear do some wonder if there is a Giver. Questions emerge with greater clarity and impulse: How did the blessings get there in the first place? Perhaps there is a higher power that has given and taken back. Why were gifts taken back? What is the meaning of my life?

All gifts demand a response. Unless a divine Giver is acknowledged, no thanks are given. Even the smallest whisper would be sufficient—two words: Thank You. Gratitude is the birth cry of all religion. It is the realization that all the blessings in one's life have been consciously, deliberately, and lovingly bestowed. When a person acknowledges this simple fact, their spirit instinctively cries out in thanksgiving. The experience of gratitude and a word of thanks is never sufficient, however, when the Giver is also one's Creator. I am the Creator. One must do more. Gratitude must be physically lifted up and returned to the higher power. Worship is the only fitting return, and it always involves sacrifice—the return of a gift to the Giver.

From the time of your first parents, worship was given to Me. Adam and Eve were grateful. They showed their gratitude by giving Me their obedience, fidelity, and trust. We were friends. I loved them. They loved Me. "I am the way and the truth and the life. No one comes to the Father except through me" (John 14:6). Eden was to be your home. In a way, they carried you as a seed with them as we took our daily strolls. They had no secrets. They felt no shame.

But then, something happened. They found another voice to trust and rejected Mine. They gave the serpent My place within their hearts. They were no longer grateful for what I offered. They wanted more and wandered into the middle of the garden in search of it. They were to learn, however, that the more they sought was not to be found in the serpent's hand, but in Me.

Your suffering has awakened your original gratitude. I am the Giver. I sent My Word, Jesus, to you like a shepherd in search of His lost sheep. My Word became flesh and made His dwelling among you. He is the light in darkness. He is the living water for those who thirst. He is the bread that satisfies. He is the answer to all you seek. He is peace. He does not give peace as the world gives it. The peace of Christ cannot even be explained fully in words but must rather be experienced through the indwelling of My Spirit.

"Cursed is the one who trusts in man, who draws strength from mere flesh and whose heart turns away from the Lord. That person will be like a bush in the wastelands; they will not see prosperity when it comes. They will dwell in the parched places of the desert, in a salt land where no one lives."

Jeremiah 17:5-6

"Here I am! I stand at the door and knock. If anyone hears my voice and opens the door, I will come in and eat with that person, and they with me" (Revelation 3:20). "Be still, and know that I am God" (Psalm 46:10). "All you who are thirsty, come to the waters; and you who have no money, come, buy and eat! Come, buy wine and milk without money and without cost. . . . Seek the Lord while he may be found; call on him while he is near" (Isaiah 55:1, 6).

My child, listen to Me. You have awakened to the Giver standing at your door. Every blessing you have known calls out for a response. Offering yourself to Me on the altar of life is the worship I seek. Nothing less will suffice. Allow the revelation of blessings to open within your spirit a seed of gratitude.

Get up from your chair and go to the door of your heart. Put your hand on the doorknob. Open. Stand face to face with My Word, Jesus. Come to Me, you who are weary. I will give you rest for your soul. I will give you a peace the world cannot give you. I am Jesus, your Savior. I am with you in the garden of your loneliness. Remember Me. I have written into every life a knock on the door, an empty tomb, a barren bush, the desert, a nightmare, or a Christmas morning so that everyone may have an opportunity to see My face and take My hand. Believe that I love you. Trust Me.

"The hour has already come for you to wake up from your slumber because our salvation is nearer now than when we first believed. The night is nearly over; the day is almost here. So let us put aside the deeds of darkness and put on the armor of light."

Romans 13:11b-12

My Prayer

"Blessed are those who keep his statutes and seek him with all their heart" (Psalm 119:2). "You are my God, and I will praise you; you are my God, and I will exalt you. Give thanks to the Lord, for he is good; his love endures forever" (Psalm 118:28-29).

Forgive me, Jesus, my Savior. I am here now. Thank You for being patient. Thank You for not giving up, for waiting. I understand now that it was You calling out during the long night. I was weary and weak. I stumbled in a thousand different ways. I fell and wallowed in self-pity. I blamed everyone but myself. I was deaf to Your pleading. I am not a victim anymore, Lord. I acknowledge Your gifts. How could

I have missed them? How could I have been so blind as not to see Your hand in my life journey? I gave my power away in so many ways, and I feel it coming back to me now, like a tide returning to shore. I feel stronger now, Lord. I put my hand on the knob, turn, and pull. I see You. I am ready to welcome You into my life.

You swooped down and grasped me in Your talons, rescued me, brought me to the golden entrance of Your sanctuary, and invited me in. I hear the mighty choir of angels singing chants of thanks and glory. You are a God rich in mercy. You are love.

I am grateful. I am grateful for all the people You chose to share my life journey: my parents, siblings, spouse, children, and grandchildren, lovers and infatuations, enemies, detractors, and destroyers. Every moment, pieced together like sentences in a story, has come together and brought me here to this moment. I am grateful for the journey and all its parts and pieces, characters, dialogue, and settings.

I am grateful for every moment of every day: for sickness and health, for food and hunger, for need and satisfaction, for joy and sadness, for success and failure, for life and death, for sin and salvation. Every part of my journey has worked to bring me here, face to face with the reality that there is a God and His name is Jesus. It is Your love within me that has given birth to my love for You. Faith begins with You, not me. You have woven the narrative, and I give You glory for my story.

You are I AM! and I am made in Your image and likeness. All glory to You, God of creation, who was and is and is to come.

Spoken in the Spirit through Jesus, the Son, to the Father. Amen.

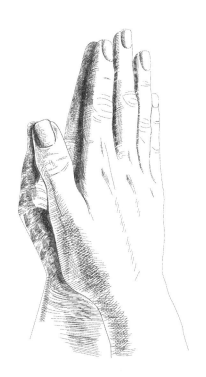

CHAPTER 6

GIVE IT ALL AWAY

God is speaking to you. Listen!

My Son, Jesus, told you, "Do not let your hearts be troubled. You believe in God; believe also in me. My Father's house has many rooms; if that were not so, would I have told you that I am going there to prepare a place for you? And if I go and prepare a place for you, I will come back and take you to be with me, that you also may be where I am. You know the way to the place where I am going" (John 14:1-4).

This world is not your home. Jesus has gone ahead to prepare a place for you in Mis kingdom. If life in the kingdom were guaranteed, you would have been born there. Why bother with earth at all if it is not a test to prove your worthiness? Why a time of preparation and testing? Because even though I chose you, you in turn must choose Me. Our marriage has been arranged, but each partner must be willing to pay the price of union. My love for you is a given, and I have proved it by My death through Jesus. You, in turn, must prove your love. This is why you are here on earth. You were made in My image and likeness, so just look into your own heart and ask yourself if what I have spoken isn't true. You wouldn't want an arranged marriage either. You want to be chosen. So, do I.

The Scripture passage I began with, John 14, was spoken to prepare the disciples for My Son's crucifixion. They needed to be reassured that with Christ's dying, His life did not end. The disciples needed to take strength from the fact that there is life beyond the grave. Jesus's kingdom is not of this world. With Jesus's death, He went ahead to Our kingdom in order to prepare a place for each of you. He promised to return and take you with Him.

The truth of the Lord's statements seems to be borne out in the many stories of people who have had near-death experiences. Almost without exception, they report seeing a light as their lives drained away. Jesus said, "I am the light of the world" (John 8:12). It is Jesus, the light, who comes to take you with Him after you finish your journey here on earth, as it happens in the case of near-death experiences. You can only assume tasks remain to be discharged if one returns before death is complete.

The fact that this earthly life is a test and preparation for life in the kingdom should challenge everyone to rethink their values. "Surely everyone goes around like a mere phantom; in vain they rush about, heaping up wealth without knowing whose it will finally be" (Psalm 39:6). The wealth of this world is not in the material. It is not what you own that should command your heart, but rather what you become.

Store up for yourselves treasure in heaven (Matthew 6:19). Jesus came among you with nothing and left the same way—in a borrowed grave. His life was not measured by what He owned, but rather by what He gave away. Your life passes like a mere vapor. You store up material treasures, all of which must be left behind. The question you should be concerned with is—"What am I giving away?" Certainly, it is a blessing to have shelter, food, family, and work you enjoy. Having material things is a blessing. Just as Jesus emptied Himself to become human, you must empty yourself to become more like Him.

It is unfortunate that some give away the wrong things. They give their power away to strangers by worrying about what others think. They loan out their bodies to those they do not love. They give away the unborn and keep the love they were meant to share. Stacks of silver grow within your silos while your brother goes hungry or your sister struggles to pay her rent.

A smile, an act of kindness, an encouraging word are all inexpensive, yet you hold them tight. Compliments and acts of compassion are left untouched and rot within your cupboards. You agree only to loan your treasures and demand return with interest. Love is the only gift you can dispense with abandon, and after you've finished giving, you find you have more than when you began.

Open your hands like Christ did on the cross and give as the Lord has given to you. Everything material must be left behind. No bank balances, properties, automobiles, articles of clothing, or designer shoes will follow you in death. "Do not store up for yourselves treasures on earth, where moths and vermin destroy, and where thieves break in and steal. But store up for yourselves treasures in heaven, where moths and vermin do not destroy, and where thieves do not break in and steal. For where your treasure is, there your heart will be also" (Matthew 6:19-21). Your clock is running. Your time is set.

Recall the story of Job. His story begins with great riches, both material and personal. Then everything he owned and everyone Job loved were brutally stripped from his life. Initially, Job's spirit is crushed, and he verges on despair. A long dialogue proceeds as he ponders the meaning of his loss.

Finally, only one blessing remains in Job's life, and it is the love of his wife. But filled with hate, she tells her husband, "Curse God and die!" (Job 2:9). Job is empty now. Even the illusion of his wife's love is stripped away.

Many at this point would despair and allow the darkness to sweep them into itself. All the scales over Job's eyes fall to the earth as he opens his heart completely to My Spirit. Job reaches up, like Peter during the raging storm, and takes My hand. Everything that has been taken is willingly surrendered to the Creator. Job knows now that all blessings, even the blessing of life itself, are only loaned.

Job proclaims, "Naked I came forth from my mother's womb, and naked I will depart. The LORD gave and the LORD has taken away; may the name of the LORD be praised" (Job 1:21). I do not allow suffering because I take pleasure in it, but rather that your heart might awaken to the hand that pours the water.

Wealthy King David discovered what was valuable only when it was taken from him at the death of Absalom, his son. Some grow in their love for Me by recognizing their blessings and turning immediately to Me with grateful hearts. Others do not recognize gifts or the Giver until they have been taken away.

"Do not hide your face from me when I am in distress. Turn your ear to me; when I call, answer

me quickly. For my days vanish like smoke; my bones burn like glowing embers. My heart is blighted and withered like grass; I forget to eat my food. In my distress, I groan aloud and am reduced to skin and bones."

Psalm 102:2-5

My hand is open. I am the Giver. If you are to live in My image, you too must open your hand and give. Jesus gave away His bread, His forgiveness, kindness, acceptance, affirmation, love, knowledge, His time, and finally, His life. The last image you have of Christ is His open hand on the cross. Jesus gave until there was nothing left to give. Until at last, He gave up His spirit.

The path to salvation is set before you. Jesus is the way. Take up your cross and follow Him. Do not cling to the things of this earth. Give while there is still time.

"A thousand years in your sight are like a day that has just gone by, or like a watch in the night. You sweep people away in the sleep of death— they are like the new grass of the morning: In the morning it springs up new, but by evening it is dry and withered."

Psalm 90:4-6

"Teach us to number our days, that we may gain a heart of wisdom."

Psalm 90:12

My Prayer

Jesus, You are the Way. It is all so simple. I am rich in many ways. Why do I make everything so complicated? Today I resolve to reflect on my blessings and discover something to give away. I begin now by offering You, Father, my thanks. I am grateful to You, Lord, for another day, breath, sight, hearing, food, and shelter. Today I resolve to give everyone I encounter a warm greeting and a smile. I will give out encouragement, a kind word, a moment of compassion. I will offer my time to the store clerk, the custodian, the person who hesitated for just that one moment, sending me a sign that she wanted to talk.

Help me, God, to live according to Your wisdom (Romans 12). Enlighten me that I might find ways to give away approval, prosperity, happiness, and peace of mind. For no reason at all, let me bring a surprise today into someone's life. I want to show people that I care about them. Help me not just to listen, but to listen attentively. Give me the ability to reflect on what I hear people saying, understand how they feel, and articulate my understanding with a heartfelt response. May I help others feel less alone. I want to care more and let others know I care.

Let me think: Is there someone for whom I can stop and pick something up at the store before I go home? Is there someone who might appreciate a card just to let them know I was thinking of them? Do I know anyone in a nursing home or a hospital? Am I putting off sending an email greeting? If I can give people a sense that I am with them, Lord, then it will make Your presence more obvious. Let people see You, Lord, when they see me.

Jesus, You asked me to give away Your teaching. I always hesitate to mention Your name to people. I don't want them to think I'm a religious fanatic, and besides, I am a little embarrassed because I really don't feel worthy to let people know I am trying to be one of Your disciples. They probably know where and how I have failed to serve You.

I need to remind myself often that You were speaking to me, Jesus, when You commanded us to go and make disciples and teach Your way of living in the world (Matthew 28). Give me the words to speak that I might plant a seed of light wherever I go. Help me be relaxed enough not just to tell people I will pray for them, but to stop in that moment and actually begin to pray. Move me to bow my head and say Your name. Give me confidence that You will provide the words that need to be spoken and heard. And if it is Your will, let it be my silence rather than my words that makes a place for Your Spirit to come forth.

"What no eye has seen, what no ear has heard, and what no human mind has conceived—the things God has prepared for those who love Him—these are the things God has revealed to us by his Spirit" (1 Corinthians 2:9-10). This world is just a brief stopover on my way home. I can't wait to see the faces of my loved ones who have already joined You! Help me to give everything away so I'll be light enough to get on the flight! Help me to be a sign of hope in something greater to others.

And there is the truth of it all—the act of giving creates one more connection within Your body on earth. Each connection weaves the tapestry of Your kingdom into the lives of Your children. Thy kingdom come, Father. Jesus prayed to You, Father: "I have given them the glory that you gave me, that they may be one as we are one—I in them and you in me—so that they may be brought to complete unity" (John 17:22-23a). Giving oneself away into the lives of others, *word by word, piece by piece, establishes communion with You, Father, as we become the body of Christ, Your Son.*

Spoken in the Spirit through Jesus, the Son, to the Father. Amen.

CHAPTER 7

LET IT GO

God is speaking. Listen!

> *"'Even now,' declares the LORD, 'return to Me
> with all your heart, with fasting and weeping
> and mourning.' Rend your heart and not your
> garments. Return to the LORD your God, for he
> is gracious and compassionate, slow to anger and
> abounding in love, and he relents from sending
> calamity,"*
>
> Joel 2:12-13

I spoke these words to the prophet Joel 400 years before I
sent My Son to earth. A frightful scourge of locusts was
upon the land, and the people saw it as an omen of their
just destruction, for they had wandered far from the way I
had shown them. When Joel spoke, the people heard My
voice, repented, and came together to pray for deliverance.
I heard their prayers and drove the locusts from their land.
Peace and prosperity were restored. It was then that I made
a promise. A day would come when I would bless the people

with much more than material things. I would send upon them My own Spirit.

"I will pour out my Spirit on all people. Your sons and daughters will prophesy, your old men will dream dreams, your young men will see visions."
Joel 2:28

After Jesus ascended to take His place at My right side, I sent My Spirit in fire and wind in fulfillment of this prophecy to Joel. The Spirit that came upon the disciples that first Pentecost remains with you to this day. The Spirit never imposes Himself on a life but rather presents Himself at the door of your heart and waits for a response. An invitation to sit at one's table must be placed before the Spirit can move in.

I will not send the Spirit where He is not welcome. You must clear a place for Him to sit. The Spirit is peace, and you can't welcome peace until you say goodbye to grief, anger, lust, revenge, hate, and greed. Sometimes hurtful experiences are welcome at your table and must be cast out before the Spirit can enter. Forgiveness is critical for the Spirit to live within you. Sometimes you are like hoarders, filling your mind and heart with so many pieces of worthless garbage that there is no room for that which can bring you true happiness—My Spirit.

Paul knew the importance of releasing yesterday's worries and creating room for the Spirit. "Let us throw off everything that hinders and the sin that so easily entangles. And let us run with perseverance the race marked out for us, fixing our eyes on Jesus, the pioneer and perfecter of faith" (Hebrews

12:1-2a). Paul fixed his mind on Christ and in Him found communion with Me, the Father.

How many times did Paul barely escape his enemies, ship-wreck, illness, or betrayal? He could have collected injuries as you collect seashells. Instead, each day, Paul chose to focus on one thing—his faith in My Son, Jesus. Jesus was the light that cast the darkness away. Jesus was the shoulder that helped Paul carry his cross and continue his mission.

Many things could be released to free a place at the table of your heart, but grief stands above them all. Grief over the death of a loved one, certainly, but also grief over the loss of a dream, a plan, a career, a marriage, a loving family. The children are raised and never bother to call or extend an invitation. Your hospital stay has no visitors. Your failure has no friends. Often it is the loss of something you only imagined was yours that stings the most. Focus on Jesus and let it all go.

How many different forms of grief have you picked up on your journey? Stop here and reflect on how this might be true. Perhaps you haven't realized what has been happening. You thought all those painful memories from the past just drifted away, disappeared, evaporated. They did not. Instead, they dug down into the deepest recesses of your mind and burrowed in like termites.

Open your memory and shuffle things around a little. Watch as your many losses rise to the surface: Pain. Rejection. Insult. Jealousy. Anger. Injustice. Vicious deeds. Reckless words. Uncontrollable rage. Lustful mistakes. Unresolved conflicts. Broken friendships. All these involve the loss of self-esteem, value, dignity, and basic goodness. Do not keep what kills.

Paul could not possibly have endured had he accumulated painful memories and stored them in his heart. One could not count Paul's wounds, yet Paul greeted every rising sun by purging his heart in order to give thanks. Grief binds one to yesterday and robs today of its joy. Release just one painful memory today and lift your heart in thanksgiving. You have My promise: the Spirit will rush in to take a seat at your table.

"If your right eye causes you to stumble, gouge it out and throw it away. It is better for you to lose one part of your body than for your whole body to be thrown into hell. And if your right hand causes you to stumble, cut it off and throw it away. It is better for you to lose one part of your body than for your whole body to go into hell."

Matthew 5:29-30

I deliberately used strong language here—"gouge it out," "cut it off," "throw it away!" It is not a hand or a foot that I'm talking about. It is the broken record of injuries your mind replays over and over again from when you were wounded. It is the feelings of inadequacy, inferiority, or shame you allowed to fester. It is the lust for more things, jealousy, and envy of the possessions or physical characteristics or popularity another enjoys. People have said things and done things to you that have been so hurtful they have actually grown into appendages on your body, just like a hand or a foot. You have fed these cancerous tumors when you should have cut them out. Why don't you realize that you are already enough for Me? "Come to me, all you who are weary and burdened, and I will give you rest" (Matthew 11:28). Come as you are!

I am here to help you let go, to heal and restore. You cannot do this on your own. The Spirit will help you. Now breathe in and hold it. Breathe out. Imagine your breath is My Spirit. Name the darkness that must be released. I alone can restore what has been lost and heal the wound torn open.

Despite all the events of your past, you must remember that I am the One who made you, and I remain pleased with My work. No one else has your fingerprints. No one else ever born will ever have your soul. You are unique—My design. If I can forget your past and renew your life each day, you must learn to accept My blessing, My forgiveness, My mercy, and My love.

All the bad things that happened to you or that you have done can be transformed into gifts, blessings even, if you allow yourself to grow in love through your experience. Suffering was permitted not to break you, but to make you the best version of yourself. I am pleased with you. Come to Me. But first—empty your hands—let go of the pain—fall into My arms. Let it all go!

My Prayer

Creator God, my heavenly Father, thank You. Thank You for imagining my soul into existence. Thank You for speaking my name into my mother's womb. Thank You for the body and mind You gave me. Thank You for the parents You chose, my spouse, siblings, and friends I have met along the way. Thank You for those who pointed me in Your direction and spoke of Jesus, Your only Son. Thank You for the moments where I failed. I am grateful. I am grateful to You, Lord.

Lord, You are right. I have been collecting memories. Most have been good, life-giving, bright memories of kindness and love, compassion and mercy. These I treasure and store away. Other memories have been traumatic, agonizing, demeaning, cancerous, and dark. I have given these negative experiences a power that must be taken back.

St. Paul learned in every defeat to release the wound and embrace the healing. He learned that in choosing You, Lord, every loss and injury could be displaced from a place of power. Instead of losing pieces of himself with every negative experience, Paul learned that in dying to himself he could be reborn again and again, constantly being shaped into a more perfect image of Your likeness.

I forget sometimes that the darkness Paul needed to release each day involved not only his own suffering but the suffering he inflicted on others. Paul ordered Christian mothers and fathers dragged away to prison and left children traumatized and abandoned. Paul stood with the mob when Stephen was stoned. Paul was the author of cruelty, wickedness, and death. He needed to give You his guilt in order to receive Your Spirit.

Spirit of God, take command of all that I have been and all that I am. Make the fire of Your love burn steady within me and give me the strength to choose to live in this world as a person of faith. You, Spirit, can melt the chains that bind me. You can take every loss and use it to make me stronger, more loving, empathetic, understanding, kind, and forgiving. Let me not be defined by what I was but by what I choose to be. Help me to be a person of faith. With the rising of the sun each morning, make me new again and continue to draw me further into communion with You, Lord of love.

I ask You now, Lord Jesus, Father, Protector, Spirit of life— purge my heart of all darkness. Expunge all that demeans my self-image; for You, Lord God, have made me good! Cut out my grief. Give me the will to let go of all "bitterness, rage and anger, brawling and slander, along with every form of malice" (Ephesians 4:31-32). Help me to be kind and compassionate, forgiving just as Christ forgave me. Restore what You have made. Help me not to grow anxious so quickly, but in all things, lead me to Your peace. Let Your Spirit flow like a river through me, Lord, and may my journey be water to this desert.

"Forget the former things; do not dwell on the past. See, I am doing a new thing! Now it springs up; do you not perceive it? I am making a way in the wilderness and streams in the wasteland . . . I, even I, am he who blots out your transgressions, for my own sake, and remembers your sins no more" (Isaiah 43:18-19, 25).

Jesus, help me fix my mind not on the past but on the present. Fix my attention on "whatever is true, whatever is noble, whatever is right, whatever is pure, whatever is lovely, whatever is admirable—if anything is excellent or praiseworthy—think about such things" (Philippians 4:8- 9). Lord, You can create anything from nothing at all. Make my mind and my life into a light. Give me hope.

Jesus, make me an empty vessel to receive Your Spirit. Take me, Lord, and make me what You first imagined. Take now my outstretched hand and lift me up as You lifted Peter from the cold waters. Walk with me, Jesus. Be my protector and shepherd. Save me.

Spoken in the Spirit through Jesus, the Son, to the Father. Amen.

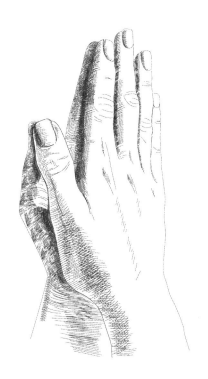

CHAPTER 8

I AM THE WORDS I SPEAK

God is speaking to you. Listen!

I t seems such a little thing, this word—Word. In the be-ginning, when all was wasteland, darkness, and abyss, I breathed My Spirit forth and spoke. My words became creation. Atoms, molecules, and photons. Stars and planets—constellations. Trillions upon trillions of heavenly bodies cast across a universe—and all of it from a word. My Word.

"Then God said: 'Let us make mankind in our image, in our likeness, so that they may rule over the fish in the sea and the birds in the sky, over the livestock and all the wild ani-mals, and over all the creatures that move along the ground.' So God created mankind in his own image, in the image of God he created them; male and female he created them" (Genesis 1:26-27). You, My child, are a word. Think hard on this truth.

When the time was fulfilled, I spoke My Word into flesh, and I became a human child—Jesus. He is the image of My invisible Being. It was I who emptied Myself and came to live among you in Him. I came so you could hear My voice more clearly. You had broken our friendship and forgotten who I was.

In the beginning, you embraced My Word, and we walked as friends through the Garden. That is, we walked together until you chose to listen to another voice. You doubted Me. You lost your trust. You rejected Me when you chose to eat the forbidden fruit. Yet, I never gave up on My creation. I came to you a second time in Jesus. Jesus is My Son. We are One. When you hear Jesus, you hear Me. He is the Word through whom all things came to be. He is the Word who brings life— eternal life. The Word is power.

You were made in My image and likeness. You were meant to model My behavior. If it is My nature to create and bring into life that which did not exist, it is part of your purpose to speak into life, to breathe forth words into being, and fill the abyss with goodness. What you say matters. "By your words you will be acquitted, and by your words you will be condemned" (Matthew 12:37). Your words count!

Your words can bring forth life or death, curse or bless, create or destroy, love or hate, build or tear down. "The tongue has the power of life and death, and those who love it will eat its fruit" (Proverbs 18:21). "A soothing tongue is a tree of life, but a perverse one crushes the spirit" (Proverbs 15:4).

Do not underestimate the good or the evil that can come from a single word. "Consider what a great forest is set on fire by a small spark. The tongue also is a fire, a world of evil among the parts of the body. It corrupts the whole body, sets the whole course of one's life on fire, and is itself set on fire by hell" (James 3:5b-6). A fire can forge wondrous works of artistry as well as destroy. "Those who consider themselves religious and yet do not keep a tight rein on their tongues deceive themselves, and their religion is worthless" (James

1:26). Satan is the father of lies (John 8:44). The Word—that is, Jesus—is truth.

Think before you speak. "The heart of the righteous weighs its answers, but the mouth of the wicked gushes evil" (Proverbs 15:28). "Set a guard over my mouth, LORD; keep watch over the door of my lips" (Psalm 141:3).

Your words spoken with love can create both light and love, matter and spirit. The Holy Spirit will help you to do this. "A good man brings good things out of the good stored up in his heart, and an evil man brings evil things out of the evil stored up in his heart. For the mouth speaks what the heart is full of" (Luke 6:45).

Never repeat gossip; even truths that detract from a person can seed darkness. "Do not slander one another" (James 4:11). "Bless those who persecute you; bless and do not curse" (Romans 12:14). "Whoever derides their neighbor has no sense, but the one who has understanding holds their tongue" (Proverbs 11:12).

You can do this: You can speak well of others. "When we put bits into the mouths of horses to make them obey us, we can turn the whole animal. Or take ships as an example. Although they are so large and are driven by strong winds, they are steered by a very small rudder wherever the pilot wants to go. Likewise, the tongue is a small part of the body, but it makes great boasts. Consider what a great forest is set on fire by a small spark. The tongue also is a fire, a world of evil among the parts of the body. It corrupts the whole body, sets the whole course of one's life on fire, and is itself set on fire by hell" (James 3:3-6). Friendships, marriages, civil harmony, betrayal, enmity, and war can all come forth from a simple word.

"Do not let any unwholesome talk come out of your mouths, but only what is helpful for building others up according to their needs, that it may benefit those who listen. And do not grieve the Holy Spirit of God, with whom you were sealed for the day of redemption. Get rid of all bitterness, rage and anger, brawling and slander, along with every form of malice. Be kind and compassionate to one another, forgiving each other, just as in Christ God forgave you" (Ephesians 4:29-32).

"But now you must also rid yourselves of all such things as these: anger, rage, malice, slander, and filthy language from your lips. Do not lie to each other, since you have taken off your old self with its practices and have put on the new self" (Colossians 3:8-10a).

It is only if the Spirit is within you that you are able to identify and name the Holy Spirit in others. When you indiscriminately label groups as bad and work hard to infer evil in their motives, be cautious, for here is the pasture where the prince of this world grazes and feasts.

Some boast that they stay home from Christian worship because all the people in the fellowship are hypocrites. This is a lie. There is goodness everywhere. When you demonize members of a political party or groups of clergy or the people in your local faith community, you walk close to the serpent, who is a liar. My goodness is everywhere, and it rests most especially on the sons and daughters of man. Be on guard against a bitter tongue. Speaking ill of others changes you. It is not uncommon for man to become the words that spill from his mouth. You underestimate your share in the divine nature.

My Prayer

Jesus, Word of God, fill me with Your Holy Spirit. Breathe Your original goodness into my heart and mind. Let me see what You see, hear what You hear. I have been living in a world of shadows when the door to Your Word could give me entrance to a world of wonder. Open the gates, Shepherd, and welcome me to Your good creation. Pour Your incantations into my mind and open my mouth that I may speak Your Word into the lives of those You have set before me. Make me into a miracle by Your Spirit.

I have spoken words of judgment, malice, condemnation, and detraction. I made no effort to search for Your finger-prints, signs of Your handiwork within others. The fact is that when I expected evil in others, I always found it! It never dawned on me that it was only the darkness within me that could call forth the darkness in others. I fed the darkness by speaking ill of individuals and groups. I lobbied hard for one political party and never hesitated to demonize the other. I proselytized for one church denomination and labored to revile others.

I deceived myself. I convinced myself that I was doing good by helping to weaken and disembowel groups outside my own. I knowingly left half-truths unchallenged. I was arrogant and proud, looking down on those who held positions different from my own. "'Teacher,' said John, 'we saw someone driving out demons in Your name and we told him to stop because he was not one of us.' 'Do not stop him,' Jesus said. 'For no one who does a miracle in my name can in the next moment say anything bad about me, for whoever is not against us is for us'" (Mark 9:38-40).

When was the last time I spoke about all the good things members of Christian traditions different from my own contributed to the common good? Do I even take the time to name what those good things might be? Yet I present myself to others as a servant of the One who is truth!

How easy it was to vilify those who are different from me. I have failed to encourage compassion for those who wander hopelessly confused as to their identity, their gender, or their faith. I spoke ill of them. The words that came forth from my mouth did not give birth to goodness, to the Light. Help me, Lord, to speak words that foster compassion, fellowship, unity, and love among all people everywhere.

Forgive me, Lord. There have been times when I searched Your garden for evil, found forbidden fruit, and was gluttonous. I not only plucked what was forbidden but also offered it to others. I have birthed evil by smearing, maligning, besmirching, misrepresenting, reviling, and vilifying others. What I did not say, I thought into existence. Pour forth Your light into me once again. Come, Spirit of Jesus, Word made flesh. Enkindle in me the fire of Your love. Let the good within me once again proclaim the goodness of Your creation and especially the goodness within every human made in Your image and likeness.

I claim You, Jesus, as my Savior. I stand in Your holy grace, Word made flesh. You are the Lamb whose blood cleanses my mind and tongue. You are my strength and the beginning of every good thing within me. I offer You my hands, my legs, and my tongue in service. Lord, send the angel who prepared Isaiah for Your work to touch my tongue. Come forth, angel of God, as You did for Isaiah. "See, this has touched your lips; your guilt is taken away and your sin atoned for" (Isaiah 6:7). May I echo Your word of forgiveness, affirmation, unity, and friendship.

Jesus, I pledge to think before I speak, to look for the good in others, to refrain from judgment, and to speak words that build, create, and breathe life. Jesus, Word of God, speak Your Holy Spirit into my being and make me new again.

Spoken in the Spirit through Jesus, the Son, to the Father. Amen.

CHAPTER 9

JESUS, I WANT TO BE YOUR FRIEND

God is speaking to you. Listen!

People struggle to know Me. Some try to approach Me as Creator. They wonder at the expanse of stars in the night sky, the clap of thunder, the changing of seasons, the birth of a child, and feel My presence. Others experience Me as King. They sense My authority in the journey of Israel and the events of their lives. Some experience Me as Father when they contemplate My part in placing food on their table, providing shelter, or the gift of health. Others see My hand in the rule of law, the commandments, the triumph of good over evil, and the foundation of civil society, coming to know Me as Judge. People relate to Me in many ways, but still, it saddens Me that only in rare moments do My children know Me as their Friend.

I want you to know Me as your friend. That is part of why I came to you as Jesus. Imagine yourself leaning over and resting your head on Jesus's shoulder as John did at the Last Supper. This is also My shoulder. Imagine it is you reaching out to take the hand of Jesus after your crippled body is healed. It is also My hand. Imagine that you are dead

Lazarus hearing the voice of Jesus calling you forth to rise from the dead. It is also My voice. Imagine that you slumber with Jesus at dinner in the home of Martha and Mary. It is My face you contemplate at the table, for Jesus and I are one. When you see Jesus, you see Me. When you hear the voice of Jesus, you hear My voice. I am your friend.

I speak when Jesus speaks. "You are my friends if you do what I command. I no longer call you servants because a servant does not know his master's business. Instead, I have called you friends, for everything that I learned from my Father I have made known to you" (John 15:14-16a). Yes, I chose you!

I want a relationship with you. I want you to know the secrets of My Spirit. I want you to hear My whispers at night. I was willing to do anything to have your friendship. I emptied Myself and came to earth for you. "Greater love has no one than this: to lay down one's life for one's friends" (John 15:13).

I made you from dust, so why would I demand perfection? I took David as My friend even with his lust. I took Moses as My friend even with his murderous temper. I took righteous Saul and James and John as friends with their thunderous anger. I took Adam and Eve as My friends knowing they would find another to take My place. I will take you just as you are, so come. Do not hesitate. I want to be your friend.

Friends do things together. They talk. It's possible to keep in touch all day, every day. They share their stories and secrets. Just be honest about why you do certain things and trust Me to understand, though I may take issue with your choices. Friends trust one another. They expect fidelity. They are in it for the long run and hang in there when they have differences or arguments or just bad feelings.

I came into a pastoral society where shepherds and sheep abounded. Everyone knew how closely shepherds kept their sheep. Everyone knew a shepherd was the only friend that counted if you were a sheep. "I am the good shepherd. The good shepherd lays down his life for the sheep" (John 10:11). The shepherd is with the sheep when the pastures are green and when the drought scorches the land and dries up the streams. The shepherd is there when the sheep are lambing and when they lie down with tetanus or black leg. I am not just a friend for the good times, but a friend for the worst times as well. You are worth My sacrifice. "Stay with me; don't be afraid . . . you will be safe with me" (1 Samuel 22:23).

Come and sit by the fire. Give Me your hand. Come to Me, you who have labored and are burdened, and allow Me to give you the rest for which you have yearned for so long (Matthew 11:28-30). I will never hurt you. I am meek and humble, so do not be afraid.

My Prayer

Father, I trust Your word that You are One with Jesus and the Spirit, even though I do not fully understand it. I hear Your voice speak to me in Revelation: "Here I am! I stand at the door and knock. If anyone hears my voice and opens the door, I will come in and eat with that person, and they with me" (Revelation 3:20).

Father, come into my body with Jesus and the Spirit. Sit with me here in this moment by the warm fire, blessing me with Your peace, Your friendship. Help me to experience in my flesh what I struggle to believe is true—that I am blessed, chosen, embraced, accepted, and understood.

Why have I lived with and carried alone so many burdens when the fact is, "I can do all this through him who gives me strength" (Philippians 4:13)? I choose to share my burdens with You, Lord and Savior. Father, You have pledged to supply my every need through Jesus (Philippians 4:19). I trust You. I am never alone. You are always at my side. Your rod and staff give me courage. You know the plan and purpose for my life. Every moment, every word, every event in history is connected to me through You. I surrender to Your love and care!

"'For I know the plans I have for you,' declares the LORD, 'plans to prosper you and not to harm you, plans to give you hope and a future. Then you will call on me and come and pray to me, and I will listen to you. You will seek me and find me when you seek me with all your heart'" (Jeremiah 29:11-13). I know I can cast all my anxieties on You because You genuinely care (1 Peter 5:7). You never fail to heal my broken heart and bind up all my wounds (Psalm 147:3). You take my suffering and through the Spirit, groan out prayers to heaven when I cannot think, let alone speak or pray (Romans 8:26). I know, "I can do all this through him who gives me strength" (Philippians 4:13). Your presence in my life sustains me and keeps me going (Psalm 73:26).

I am sorry for the times I have been embarrassed to let others know we are friends. I know how I would feel if others did that to me. I regret that, especially given what I know this relationship has cost You. Never let me be ashamed to pray in public, to repeat what You have said, to let others know where You live and how You can be found. I should be sharing You instead of hiding You away. I should be telling others all You have done for me. You encouraged me when I felt defeated; strengthened me when I wanted to give up.

You healed me when I was broken. You saved me over and over again when I tumbled and fell.

You've already told me how I can show how much I value Your friendship: "If you love me, keep my commands" (John 14:15). Your command is that I love You and my neighbor with my heart, my soul, and mind. I'm working on that, Lord (Matthew 22:37-39).

Friend. You are my Friend. You are my best Friend. A cacophony of voices is vying for my attention, so Lord, help me fix my attention on Your voice above all others. "You have the words of eternal life" (John 6:68). Help me to focus, concentrate, listen, understand, and obey Your Word. I pray I may be a worthy friend, willing to trust, to hope, and to endure whatever comes.

Spoken in the Spirit through Jesus, the Son, to the Father. Amen.

CHAPTER 10

DO NOT LET YOUR HEARTS BE TROUBLED

God is speaking to you. Listen!

"Do not let your hearts be troubled. You believe in God; believe also in me."

John 14:1

If you are "troubled," then hearing Me say, "Do not be troubled" may cause you to feel very frustrated. How do you turn off anxiety when someone is driving at 75 miles per hour three feet from your rear bumper? How do you just stop worrying when there is no money in your purse for food when you have children?

Remember that I am the One who made you, so I know how your body and mind work. It is impossible for a normal person to just turn off anxiety! Anxiety is often a response to a very real and threatening situation. You should be troubled and anxious in certain circumstances. You may study harder if you are anxious about a test, watch your diet if you are anxious about your health, or be more vigilant in checking the car seat for the baby. Anxiety may motivate you to take water on a hike, stop smoking, watch your tongue, or work harder.

It is when anxiety becomes extreme and habitual without a necessary connection to a real or impending threat that it is not only unhealthy but deadly. It is to this experience that I say, "Do not worry about tomorrow, for tomorrow will worry about itself. Each day has enough trouble of its own" (Matthew 6:34). There is a point at which you need to stop thinking you can rectify every situation and let Me step into your life and take over. You can't concentrate on two different things at the same time: your troubles or Me.

When your anxiety is weighing on your heart and affecting your quality of life, you need to make an important decision. You need to choose, decide, and force yourself to focus on your blessings, your gifts. Remind yourself that I am here and entrust yourself into My care.

The apostle Paul had every reason to live as a troubled, anxious, angry, and negative man. He was party to murder and homelessness. He was a victim of shipwreck, stoning, and beatings, bitten by snakes, betrayed, rejected, driven out of cities, and locked in prison. If Paul began each day reliving all the bad things that he had done or that had happened to him, he would have been a miserable man, incapable of functioning, let alone traveling the world to preach. He had a valid argument were he to define himself as a victim. Paul rejected victimhood in favor of being a victor. Considering yourself a powerless victim is unworthy of your gift of the Holy Spirit.

Each day when Paul opened his eyes, he turned his mind to Me. He thought immediately of his blessings, mustered up the faces of the friends he had made, and recalled moments of grace. Paul lived in the Spirit. Paul chose Me not once, but every day, and sometimes every hour of every day. He lived in the light. This is why Paul could sing hymns in prison, calmly pray with strangers during a storm, and get up after having been beaten by a mob and walk thirty miles to the next village to preach My Word.

Set your mind on Jesus and His many blessings. Choose to be positive. Trust in the Lord. "Set your mind on things above, not on earthly things" (Colossians 3:2). "For the Spirit God gave us does not make us timid, but gives us power, love, and self-discipline" (2 Timothy 1:7). Engage self-control. You cannot choose your feelings, but you can choose your thoughts. In every circumstance, fix your thoughts on My Son, Jesus. He is the rock. He is the light. He is your salvation.

Paul was a great pupil. He learned from Christ how to live in peace. "Rejoice in the Lord always. I will say it again: Rejoice! Let your gentleness be evident to all. The Lord is near. Do not be anxious about anything, but in every situation, by prayer and petition, with thanksgiving, present your requests to God. And the peace of God, which transcends all understanding, will guard your hearts and your minds in Christ Jesus" (Philippians 4:4-6). Paul practiced what he preached.

The key to fixing a troubled heart is to focus your mind on Christ, My Son, and on your blessings, goodness, and love. Paul invites you to pray "with thanksgiving." Never forget that no matter what may be going wrong in your life, you are immeasurably blessed. You have no power over other people or what happens to you in this world. You do, however, have power over your response to people and your experiences. Your response must be a self-willed, deliberate choice to fix your mind on blessings, signs of My presence, and love. Do this and the Spirit will breathe peace through you. And you will sing.

"For the Spirit God gave us does not make us timid, but gives us power, love, and self-discipline" (2 Timothy 1:7). My peace surpasses all understanding. My peace makes no sense to those around you. My peace will fix your troubled heart. Like a mother bird, you shall dwell beneath My wings. "Come to me, all you who are weary and burdened, and I will give you rest" (Matthew 11:28).

My Prayer

Jesus, I consistently find myself overwhelmed. People die, plans fall apart, and burdens weigh me down. I see no way forward. Living is too hard. I am weary of the journey. Just getting out of bed some mornings can be a challenge, let alone going to work and putting on a smile.

When things are not going well, I have a major problem experiencing Your presence. When I am riddled with anxiety, little else seems to exist but the problem at hand. Am I a bad Christian so that You don't seem to hear my plea and make my burden light? Do I deserve my misery? Have You planned this punishment like a prison sentence and I just have to wait till the time of chastisement has passed? All my efforts at finding relief seem to be in vain. Nothing I do seems to make a difference.

You tell me that these troubles are tests. I hear You, Lord, "Do not conform to the pattern of this world, but be transformed by the renewing of your mind. Then you will be able to test and approve what God's will is—his good, pleasing, and perfect will" (Romans 12:2). Instead of collapsing into depression or negative thinking when I feel oppressed, I need to reflect on the good You might bring forth from the experience. I need to see every challenge as an opportunity to grow.

"Consider it pure joy, my brothers and sisters, whenever you face trials of many kinds, because you know that the testing of your faith produces perseverance. Let perseverance finish its work so that you may be mature and complete, not lacking anything" (James 1:2-4).

"Suffering produces perseverance; perseverance, character; character, and character hope" (Romans 5:3-5). Suffering, indeed, every trial is an opportunity to go to You, Lord, and to choose trust. The Spirit is offered as a gift, but it's up to me to receive the gift, treasure it, and use it. Yes, sometimes troubles seem to be overwhelming, but nothing can really stop me from taking control of my thoughts. I must decide to list my blessings. I can choose to speak words of thanks and step outside the experience of victimhood, of misery.

Jesus, from this moment forward, every time I feel anxious or depressed, miserable or trapped, overwhelmed and powerless before my troubles, I will gather my resolve and make a choice. I will deliberately turn my mind to blessings, to Your gifts, to thankfulness. You have been good to me, Lord. I will choose to be grateful. Gratitude is the song in the prison. Gratitude is the prayer in the storm, the light in the darkness. If I put hot water in a bucket filled with ice-cold water, the mixture changes. It is no longer a bucket of cold water. If I pour gratitude in where there is anxiety, my feelings change, my perspective clarifies, and my will to go forward returns.

I know, Jesus, that gratitude is more than positive thinking. Gratitude is where all religion, all journeys to You begin. Gratitude makes the barrier between this world and Your kingdom thin. Gratitude ushers in more positive emotions, sanctions relationships, diminishes adversity, and improves health. Gratitude is the first sign the Holy Spirit has answered my summons!

Lord Jesus, I choose to fix my mind on Your power, Your plan, and Your abiding love for me.

"You, LORD, are my lamp; the LORD turns my darkness into light" (2 Samuel 22:29). Yes!

"The Lord is close to the brokenhearted and saves those who are crushed in spirit" (Psalm 34:18).

"Cast all your anxiety on him because he cares for you" (1 Peter 5:7).

"The LORD himself goes before you and will be with you; he will never leave you nor forsake you. Do not be afraid; do not be discouraged" (Deuteronomy 31:8).

Jesus, my Friend, I recall the story of Job. Everyone Job loved (and he had many children and grandchildren) and everything Job owned (he owned much) was brutally taken from him. Last of all, Job lost his health and the love of his wife. While Job was seated on a pile of dung and covered with sores, his wife told Job to "Curse God and die!" (Job 2:9).

At this point in his story, Job appears to have nothing. He seems to have no one. Job has no power over what has just transpired. The events of his life cannot be undone.

His children and grandchildren are no longer among the living. Job turns his mind to You, Father. You are the Light. He surrenders his questions, his pain, his grief, his misery into Your care. Job's response to his experience of emptiness is to lift his heart and mind to You. He turns his loss into a sacrificial offering. He gives everyone and everything over to Your hands. It is now that the Holy Spirit wells up within him. He knows in the depths of his being that he has never been alone or abandoned.

Job's loss was initially the cause of his misery, but then he remembers You, Father. You, gracious Lord, willed those blessings into Job's life. You are good. Job's life has been wonderful. Your kind and merciful hand had always been with him. Job turns his thoughts away from his troubles to Your love, Father. Gratitude gives birth to peace. Gratitude opens the floodgates into the ocean of Your grace. Your Holy Spirit rushes in with fire and wind. You, Creator, are the source of all Job's blessings. You are good. He knows You have loved him his entire life and You love him still. Job feels safe, secure, and is filled with hope. He is at peace.

"Naked I came from my mother's womb, and naked I will depart. The LORD gave and the LORD has taken away; may the name of the LORD be praised" (Job 1:21).

Job's circumstances have not changed. His children and grandchildren are still dead. He is still covered with sores. His wife blames and despises him. Even now, he has no one and nothing. But he has You, Father! His mind is fixed on You, Lord. He is at peace.

Jesus, I surrender my troubles, my anxiety, my unhappiness, and my depression into Your care. I imagine standing before You holding a platter and on that platter is all that afflicts me. I lift the platter before You. You extend Your open hands. You take the platter from me. I surrender my problems, anxiety, misery, depression, financial problems, relationships, job, hopes, and dreams into Your care.

You brought me here to Your feet, Lord. Thank You. Thank You even for the problems. You give. You take away. This world is not my destination, only a stopover. It is all temporary. I am grateful, Father-Creator. "Father, if you are willing, take this cup away from me; still, not my will, but yours be done" (Luke 22:42). Nothing that is said to me or done to me at this point will rob me of Your peace, Jesus. I choose to live one day at a time in Your grace. Thank You! I am grateful. Amen.

All glory to You, Jesus, My Savior. I love You!

Spoken in the Spirit through Jesus, the Son, to the Father. Amen.

CHAPTER 11

DELIVER US FROM EVIL

God is speaking to you. Listen!

I am the mother bird who calls you to safety beneath My wing. "You are my hiding place; You will protect me from trouble and surround me with songs of deliverance" (Psalm 32:7).

There is a reason Scripture calls the serpent (Genesis 3:1) the deceiver (Revelation 12:9), tempter (Matthew 4:3), Beelzebub, the prince of demons (Matthew 12:24), evil one (1 John 5:18), enemy (Matthew 13:9), liar and murderer (John 8:44), angel of light (2 Corinthians 11:14), Belial (2 Corinthians 11:14), devil (Matthew 4:1), god of this age (2 Corinthians 4:4), a roaring lion (1 Peter 5:8), and accuser (Revelation 12:10). It has many names because it has many faces, many voices, and takes on many, many disguises!

You are being hunted. Its eyes are fixed on you. It is hungry. I am the Lord, and there is no other God besides Me. Come and take shelter beneath My wings. Your journey has awakened the darkness. Your love for the Spirit has echoed into the chambers of the abyss. Why did you think for one moment that the voice that spoke to Jesus in the garden had been extinguished?

Sometimes it is one. Sometimes they are many. They have many identities and take on many disguises. Sometimes they stand apart from you. Most often, they speak from within.

These entities are fixed on what they see as a great and wondrous return to the past, to the chaos from which creation was called forth. Evil appears first in the human story when Adam and Eve were visited in Eden. Satan came to Gethsemane to offer My Son another path than that which had been chosen. It came to Paul many times as he worked to preach My kingdom. It comes to every pastor in every time who fishes to fill My nets. It comes to every soul born of the Spirit. It has come to you. It will not leave until you have drawn your last breath and part this sweet earth where it is the celebrated prince.

Evil describes the spirit that defined and moved the cruelest among you—psychopaths and murderers like Lenin, Stalin, Hitler, Sui Yang Di, and Pol Pot. Evil feeds on racism, greed, hate, and revenge. It rejoices in envy and jealousy, breeding discontent when someone else has more. It arrives with a smile, a gracious word of compliment, an invitation to friendship, a word of scripture. It takes on the mask of kindness, compassion, religion, patience, and goodwill. Evil often boasts of its love for Me and for My work. It pretends to want justice, a wolf in the clothing of a lamb. Innocent. Harmless. Pleasant to look at. Nonthreatening. But poisonous and deadly.

When Satan is busy with you, I try to intervene. I whisper to your heart, and if you listen, you begin to doubt what you hear from Satan. You must remember you have been bought with the blood of Christ, and the Spirit is within you. You are not alone in this battle. "You, dear children, are from God and have overcome them, because the one who is in you is greater than the one who is in the world" (1 John 4:4). Do not, however, be overconfident. Satan never left Christ while He walked the earth, so be assured he will not give up on you.

There is always one sure test for spiritual darkness: Does it give birth to love? "Love comes from God. Everyone who loves has been born of God and knows God. Whoever does not love does not know God, because God is love. This is how God showed his love among us: He sent his one and only Son into the world that we might live through him" (1 John 4:7-9).

Love brings peace, unity, and understanding. Love draws people together. Love works to affirm the good, thinks the best of others, builds, boosts confidence, reassures, strengthens, and invigorates. Evil looks for the blemish, the stain, the fracture, and seeks to divide. Test this voice by asking yourself if it makes you feel peace with others, strengthens the bonds between you, and fosters understanding. Does it motivate you to recommit to service or move you to withdraw?

My Son spoke many words when He walked among you, but allow Me to draw your attention to these: "For where two or three gather in my name, there am I with them" (Matthew 18:20). Coming together threatens the spiritual forces of evil. The togetherness and integrity of your body, mind, soul, family, marriage, church fellowship, financial security, and friendship are objects of evil's scorn. Evil never tires in its assault. It seeks to return all to dust and dust to the void. It is part of every mental and physical illness, financial ruin, betrayal, divorce, murder, trauma, word of gossip, and war. Evil pulls apart. It divides.

Breaking the woven tapestry of all creation is the primary focus of evil, for what God has brought together from the sea of chaos must be torn asunder and returned to the void. These forces of darkness feast on brokenness, division, and chaos. They are irrational by definition.

Above all the treasures I, Your Creator, have wrought, one stands above all, and that is the fellowship of believers. This triumph over evil brings people into communion with Christ's divinity. Humanity, once broken apart, becomes the Body of Christ. "For where two or three gather in my name, there am I with them" (Matthew 18:20). Jesus came to bring the human family together. The purest form of worship is communal. Give us this day our daily bread. Deliver us from evil. When Christians come together, there is Christ. Your communion with others and with Me is the antithesis of evil.

"Be alert and of sober mind. Your enemy the devil prowls around like a roaring lion looking for someone to devour. Resist him, standing firm in the faith, because you know that the family of believers throughout the world is undergoing the same kind of sufferings. And the God of grace, who called you to his eternal glory in Christ, after you have suffered a little while, will himself restore you and make you strong, firm, and steadfast. To him be the power forever and ever. Amen" (1 Peter 5:8-11).

"The thief comes only to steal and kill and destroy; I have come that they may have life and have it to the full. I am the good shepherd; I know my sheep, and my sheep know me" (John 10:10-11).

"Put on the full armor of God, so that you can take your stand against the devil's schemes. For our struggle is not against flesh and blood, but against the rulers, against the authorities, against the powers of this dark world and against the spiritual forces of evil in the heavenly realms" (Ephesians 6:11-12). I say do not be afraid, for "I am with you and will rescue you" (Jeremiah 1:8). "Never will I leave you; never will I forsake you" (Hebrews 13:5). I am the Good Shepherd.

Jesus taught you to pray, "And lead us not into temptation, but deliver us from the evil one" (Matthew 6:13). Do not minimize this threat. Do not persuade yourself that evil as a conscious being with ill designs does not exist or concern itself with you. On the other hand, a word of caution—Do not give it too much of your attention! Instead, pour all your attention on the Light. Work hard to draw your mind to the blessings that surround you and Me, the giver, I Am. Search and name the goodness of all those I bring into your circle. Tell them of the good you see. Complement one another. Be confident and positive in the face of every obstacle or hardship. Live in hope. Seek Jesus, My Son, for He can be found (Isaiah 55:6-7). He is with you and within you. Stand in the Holy Spirit and speak His Holy name. Jesus. Seek the good in one another and name it.

My Prayer

Jesus, my Savior, hear my prayer. Draw my hardened heart into Your circle of grace.

What a struggle it is to turn away from being critical and negative! If someone with a white dress stands before me, how can I not be drawn to stare at the black spot on it and ignore the dress? I acknowledge before You, Lord, that I have stared at the stain and ignored the person wearing the garment. Truth be told, very often, I do not even try to look into a stranger's heart, hold it in my hands, or reverence its beat. The black spot pulls me in. I examine the fault, the brokenness, the sin, and fail to see the human spirit that carries it. I see first the broken law and fail to look deeper into the journey of the one who broke it. I perceive the negative, the detraction, and broken rule in another and let slip away any reflection on the same person's anguish and failure to thrive. Compassion demands that I stand within another's experience, and I find it easier to stand apart. Building Your kingdom is work, and I am often lazy.

Yet, sometimes I think of myself as a crusader in service to Jesus. You must see how hard I labor in the cause. But instead of focusing all my energy on the mission, I find myself turning on the soldiers beside me. I fix my mind on their corrupt motivations, their compromised commitment, their false way of living, their poor choices, and clear evidence of pollution. I am drawn more and more into what detracts, divides, and degrades. I convince myself that they are no more than hypocrites, and I would do well to go it alone, to disassociate. Community is difficult.

The questions that afflict me make me pause to consider whether the prince of this world hasn't been shaping my thoughts. "Why do I have to worship with others? Who made the pastor an authority? Christ cannot be party to this wretched crowd of stupid misfits who make so many errors in judgment and so much a mess of their lives! I must leave this fellowship. I can pray alone and serve alone."

How proud and arrogant is this posture of omniscience. These are the fruits of evil—division and brokenness. Christ calls people together, to accept one another's faults, and to build fellowship. We need one another. I need others.

There is no Christianity without the cross. The hand separated from the body withers. Your Spirit, Jesus, brought me to fellowship, and I beseech this same Spirit to keep me there. It is precisely with those who fail at living the teaching of Jesus but try nonetheless that I can be made humble, nurtured, and healed. It is the weakest who, in Christ, can make me strong. It is the broken body that, in Christ, can make me whole. It is by listening to the least and lowest but honest and righteous that I will meet truth and find wisdom. There are no perfect people in Christ's family, only sinners. This is where I belong. In fellowship. Together. I am a sinner in need, and they are my brothers and sisters. We are all washed in the blood of the Lamb. I am unworthy to be seated with them at the altar, but in their compassion, they have offered me a seat at their table. Together, in communion, we share the bread of life and inherit the promise of Christ.

Jesus, I now commit myself to fellowship with other Christians. You have planted the good in each person, and it will be my work to discover and name it. I know now that every white garment has a black spot, including my own. Father, deliver me from evil and bind me to the fellowship of Your disciples. Make us one in Christ. May I learn not to see loose threads and pull the tapestry apart, but rather to seek ways to weave the threads together. Help me to commit to build and affirm the good in others, lead them to the waters of life, and encourage them to drink. May all I do give strength to the body of Christ. May all its broken parts be made whole.

Glory to You, Father, Son, and Spirit, now and forever.

Spoken in the Spirit through Jesus, the Son, to the Father. Amen.

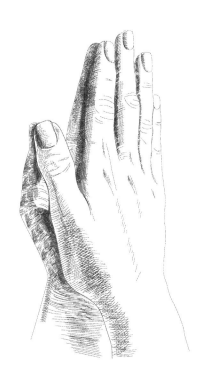

CHAPTER 12

JESUS WEPT

God is speaking to you. Listen!

"Jesus wept" (John 11:35). That's the shortest sentence in the Bible. Jesus, My Son, the Lamb of God, wept. St. John has a vision of Jesus as the Lamb seated on His heavenly throne, surrounded by hosts of angels. It is promised that Jesus, the Lamb, will "wipe away every tear from their eyes" (Revelation 7:17). This Jesus who cried is the same Jesus who, as the Word, generated all of creation. It is through Him all things came into being (John 1:3).

This man with tears is about to tell Martha that He is Himself the resurrection and the life, and whoever believes in Him will never die (John 11:25), and still, He wept! No human will ever have the absolute certainty Jesus did that there is life beyond this world, yet Jesus wept. Being who He was and knowing what He knew, if Jesus could still weep over the death of Lazarus, the message is clear. I, your God, know your pain and suffering. Jesus is one with Me, and I am one with Him. I see your anguish and promise to take your pain away.

Grief does not speak of your lack of faith; rather, grief speaks of the depth of your love. Jesus loved Lazarus. You love someone too! An unborn child, an infant, a spouse, a parent, sibling, or friend—each loss is different. Each "goodbye" has its own blade. Each death has its own unique sorrow.

Even though the Bible is full of promises of life beyond the grave, you, a believer, still ask for a sign. You need reassurance. Fear is death's sister. It is terrifying to contemplate the death of your relationships, the end of love, because you are your relationships. You are the connections you have made with others. Death forces you to rethink who you are in the world because a piece of yourself seems to be lost. Life without love can be worse than death itself. Jesus wept. I, Your Father, understand.

The message of Scripture concerning the afterlife can be confusing at times, for the Bible records under one cover the equivalent of two thousand years of revelation. Abraham believed in many gods, and it took centuries for My people to understand there is only one God. It also took centuries of revelation before My chosen people understood that I made man to live forever. Eternal life in My kingdom was always My plan. Jesus is the final word of revelation on the existence of a place prepared for each of you after your life on earth.

Early in the history of My revelation, some believed in Sheol, where the dead slept in an eternal coma of life without life. "For the living know that they will die, but the dead know nothing; they have no further reward, and even their name is forgotten" (Ecclesiastes 9:5). Abraham, the father of your faith, was dead for over 1,800 years when Christ came to clarify the truth once and for all time as to what lies beyond the grave.

Jesus, the Word, is truth. There is no Sheol, no abode of the dead where the dead sleep in an everlasting coma. Heaven, My kingdom, is home to many forms of sentient beings. Jesus made our divine invitation to share immortality certain.

With Jesus's teaching, you now know that all humankind will face a last judgment. Those who have repented of their sins, given their lives to Jesus, and gratefully accepted His full and complete payment for their sins will enter My kingdom. I promise a world where there will be no more death or suffering, only perfect peace. "Never will I leave you; never will I forsake you" (Hebrews 13:5). "I am with you always, to the very end of the age" (Matthew 28:20). I am with you now!

Grief can be savage and without mercy, crumbling even those with great faith. It can be like a black hole, a star that collapses upon itself, consuming surrounding stars and planets in its immeasurable gravity. My Spirit is stronger than the black hole, and it is My Spirit who comes upon you when you humbly open Scripture and listen for My voice. As you begin to pray, imagine I have My arm around your shoulders and pull you close to Myself. The Spirit was sent precisely for your comfort and surety where there is turmoil and confusion. Stand in the power of Jesus's Word and affirm the truth of life beyond the grave. Jesus promised never to leave you or forsake you. He promised to come back and take you to a new home He has prepared in My kingdom.

St. Paul told you that as long as you are in the corruptible body, you are away from the Lord. My Son will change that corruptible body in the blinking of an eye at the sound of the last trumpet, and you will be raised. Recall once again Jesus' words to Martha, where He said, "I am the resurrection and the life. The one who believes in me will live, even though they die; and whoever lives by believing in me will never die" (John 11:25-26). Draw your attention to the word never. The souls of the just do not exist in an eternal sleep. You are defined by your memories, your communion with others, and with Me. An eternal sleep would be no better than death, and I have promised eternal life. Believe that My love does not end. The people you love will not end.

Jesus spoke from the cross to the repentant thief, "Truly I tell you, today you will be with me in paradise" (Luke 23:43). Jesus did not tell the man "you will be with Me at the resurrection after the last judgment." Jesus said you will be with Me today!

Your true home is yet to come, that is, after you die. "Therefore we are always confident and know that as long as we are at home in the body, we are away from the Lord" (2 Corinthians 5:6). When you leave the body, you are welcomed home, to My kingdom. Yes, you are not fully restored until your body rises at the general resurrection at the final judgment, but your spirit, your consciousness, is with Me. Love does not die.

The Scriptures tell you that the dead are not only with Me, but they continue to see you whom they left behind. Would any of us be the same person if our individual memories, our connections to others, were erased? Would the repentant thief who was promised paradise be the same person if knowledge of his children and wife and siblings was no more? No, Jesus said, "You will be with me in paradise." Jesus did not say a shell of who you are now will be with Me in paradise. He said, You!

Just as My self-definition is a triune relationship, you who are human are defined by your communion with others and with Me. Love does not die (1 Corinthians 13:8). To cut the unique memories from the mind of your departed loved ones would be equivalent to erasing their lives. It would be no different from death. Jesus was clear that there is a promised eternal life for individual persons.

Recall the visions of St. John recorded in the book of Revelation. John glimpses heaven. He reports seeing what he describes as living creatures, angels, and saints ("holy ones"). The saints in heaven were men and women like you. And what are the saints doing in heaven? They are lifting up prayers that rise like incense before My throne.

This scene would ring familiar with Jews, who had worshiped in the Jerusalem temple, for that temple is the mirror of the heavenly sanctuary. The Jerusalem temple had an altar dedicated to the burning of incense. The cloud of smoke was a visible symbol of all the prayers offered on behalf of the Jewish people. John's vision confirms a similar scene taking place in heaven itself at this very moment.

"Another angel, who had a golden censer, came and stood at the altar. He was given much incense to offer, with the prayers of all God's people, on the golden altar in front of the throne. The smoke of the incense, together with the prayers of God's people, went up before God from the angel's hand."

Revelation 8:3-4

St. John tells us this cloud is the prayers of God's people. These are not only the prayers of the living rising from the Jerusalem temple, but the prayers offered in heaven itself by the holy ones, the saints, angels, and living creatures standing before God's throne.

What on earth would the saints in heaven be praying for, but for those they loved while on earth? They remember you. Their love endures. They see your pain as do I, your Father. They pray for your peace, your comfort (Jeremiah 15:1; Revelation 5:8).

Recall Jesus' transfiguration witnessed by Peter, James, and John on Mt. Tabor. These apostles saw with their own eyes Moses and Elijah conversing with Jesus. These saints were conscious, not asleep, and it is obvious if they are able to have a conversation with Jesus, that their individuality remains intact. If Moses and Elijah could converse with Jesus when they were dead, then why wouldn't your loved ones who have been baptized with the Holy Spirit be able to speak to the Lord? Would it not make perfect sense, given what John wrote in Revelation, to conclude that they are lifting up prayers on your behalf?

Jesus has promised that there would be much more to be revealed than what was recorded in Scripture, and it would be the promised Spirit who would guide you into all the truth (John 16:12-13). Ask the Spirit if your loved ones see you right now and pray for you. Your communion with your loved ones survives the grave.

"Love never fails. But where there are prophecies, they will cease; where there are tongues, they will be stilled; where there is knowledge, it will pass away. For we know in part, and we prophesy in part, but when completeness comes, what is in part disappears. . . . Love never fails" (1 Corinthians 13:8-10).

My Prayer

Holy Spirit, come forth. Burst out from the chamber of my heart where You dwell within me. Be manifest, Spirit of peace, Comforter. Attend to my suffering and be merciful. Pour the blood of Jesus that destroyed sin and death upon my head. Burst Your light upon my doubt and burn it away. Baptize me with the living waters of Your Spirit and confirm me in the truth of Christ's Word of eternal life. Attend to the darkness that haunts my mind and make Your truth clear.

With the conviction of the Holy Spirit, I stand in the teaching of Christ and profess the resurrection to be real. I wipe my tears from my cheeks and the sadness from my heart. I claim the strength and power of Jesus, the Lamb. I call forth the Spirit I received when I first proclaimed Jesus as my Savior to bring me the promised hope, comfort, and peace. Be present with me, Spirit of Jesus. Hold me. Forgive me. Reassure me. Help me to be confident in the resurrection and life beyond the grave. Take away my doubt and fear.

Thank You, Jesus. Thank You for taking our sins away through Your death on the cross and resurrection. Thank You for opening the gates of heaven to those who claim You as Savior. Thank You for going ahead to prepare a place for each of us. Thank You, Jesus, for the promise of Your future return. Thank You for the resurrection and gift of a glorified body at the end of the age. All glory and blessing be upon You, Lord Jesus. Thank You, Jesus, for reassuring me that neither my love nor memories nor the love and memories of my dearly departed will end (1 Corinthians 13).

Jesus, thank You for counting my loved ones among the holy ones before Your throne. Thank You for allowing them to keep their memories, their personalities, and all the uniqueness of the gift they were and continue to be. Thank You for sustaining their love and making it pure and holy and more now, having joined with You, than it ever was on earth. Thank You for allowing my loved ones to continue to share my life as I make my own journey toward the gates of Your kingdom.

Hear their prayers on my behalf and renew Your Spirit within me each day. Thank You for healing their spirits in death, and thank You for the promise that You will raise their glorified bodies in the general resurrection at the last judgment. Thank You, Father, for the angels who offer prayers for all of us.

I give You glory, Father, as I lift up my voice now and join the hosts of heaven. "Holy, holy, holy is the Lord God Almighty, who was, and is, and is to come" (Revelation 4:8). "Amen! Praise and glory and wisdom and thanks and honor and power and strength be to our God for ever and ever. Amen!" (Revelation 7:12).

Spoken in the Spirit through Jesus, the Son, to the Father. Amen.

CHAPTER 13

YOUR LIFE IS A MIST

God is speaking to you. Listen!

"The world and its desires pass away, but whoever does the will of God lives forever."

1 John 2:17

Were your days as numerous as the grains of sand on the shore, you might treat them with disregard. Only what is scarce is truly cherished. Your life is designed to be brief so that you may learn to treasure each moment. "You do not know what tomorrow will bring. What is your life? You are a mist that appears for a little time and then vanishes" (James 4:14). "My days are like the evening shadow; I wither away like grass" (Psalm 102:11).

"Lord, you have been our dwelling place throughout all generations. Before the mountains were born or you brought forth the whole world, from everlasting to everlasting you are God. You turn people back to dust, saying, 'Return to dust, you mortals.' A thousand years in your sight are like a day that has just gone by, or like a watch in the night. Yet you sweep people away in the sleep of death—they are like the new grass of the morning: In the morning it springs up new, but by evening it is dry and withered" (Psalm 90:1-6).

"Night is coming" (John 9:4). The brevity of your life is, in itself, a gift. It compels you to ponder the present and yearn for a future with Me. I did not pull your spirit from a heavenly vault of sleeping souls and place it in a body on earth. You were never an angel. You had no life before the one you now live. And you will not return for another life on earth in another body. You will be judged after your one life on earth, and that judgment will seal your eternal fate. Your spirit did not exist until I fashioned your body within your mother's womb.

Jesus promised eternal life to those who accept Him as Lord and Savior, keep the commandments, and love Me and their neighbor. But Jesus never said "ONLY." As if only those who meet these requirements will enter My kingdom. Moses and Elijah appeared with Jesus at His Transfiguration, and they had received the gift of eternal life, yet they never professed Jesus as their Lord and Savior. He had not yet come into the world. Your unborn or unbaptized children never had the chance to learn of My Son's coming. Should they be confined to hell through no fault of their own? Your faith in Jesus and the gift of the Holy Spirit is My ultimate gift, for which you must always be grateful. But do not presume to know the limits of My love. Do not tell Me who is worthy or unworthy of eternal life.

Not every human being born will enter My kingdom. There will be a general judgment at the end of time where the sheep and the goats will be separated. Consider this: What if your spirit ended with the death of your body? If you are dust, who would dare condemn Me, your Creator, for allowing you to return to the dust, to nothingness, to the abyss, to not being? I do not owe you eternity any more than I owed you the life you've been privileged to share. Should I feel obligated to fashion a tomorrow for someone who was never grateful for today? Should I be bound to continue to send gifts to a creature who refused to thank Me for gifts received? Should I reward those who feasted while remaining indifferent to their brothers' and sisters' misery?

Man and woman, you are dust, and to dust, you will return. The grass withers, the mist is burned away in the sunshine. Do not fear hell! Fear nonexistence. Fear the formless emptiness of chaos. The notion of not being remembered in the minds of the living is a shallow concept of death. Fear the end of your existence, your blotting out from an infinite universe. This is the original, primal fear shared by every sentient creature.

Any person true to themselves would prefer burning in hell to annihilation, the great return to nothing, the negation of all you are, nonexistence! Yet despite the truth revealed by Jesus, people remain arrogant and proud, claiming as truth whatever flavor of teaching the prince of this world is serving from one year to the next.

"(The LORD) knows how we are formed; he remembers that we are dust. The life of mortals is like grass, they flourish like a flower of the field; the wind blows it and it is gone, and its place remembers it no more. But from everlasting to everlasting the LORD's love is with those who fear him, and his righteousness with their children's children—with those who keep his covenant and remember to obey his precepts."

Psalm 103:14-18

"In their hearts humans plan their course, but the LORD establishes their steps" (Proverbs 16:9). I chose you to hear the Name of Jesus. His Name is above every other name. "That at the name of Jesus every knee should bow, in heaven and on earth and under the earth, and every tongue acknowledge that Jesus Christ is Lord, to the glory of God the Father" (Philippians 2:10-11).

You have heard the living Word speak. "I am the way and the truth and the life. No one comes to the Father except through me. If you really know me, you will know my Father as well. From now on, you do know him and have seen him" (John 14:6-7). Jesus told you, "I am the resurrection and the life. The one who believes in me will live, even though they die; and whoever lives by believing in me will never die" (John 11:25-26).

Do you think I will overlook those who reject Jesus and welcome them to sit beside the angels and holy ones in My kingdom? Do you think I will turn My head and pretend I do not hear the contempt with which My Son's name is spat out with indifferent laughter? "I know your deeds, that you are neither cold nor hot. I wish you were either one or the other! So, because you are lukewarm—neither hot nor cold—I am about to spit you out of my mouth" (Revelation 3:15-16). Those who turn away from the sacrifice of My Son on the cross with indifference have My permission to return from whence they came; in this way, each shall be their own judge.

But to those born of His name, I will summon you forth from this world into a new creation through the Spirit. To those who receive His teaching with reverence and strive to walk His holy way, I open the gates of My kingdom. To those who proclaim His name with blessing in worship and bring their children to the path of righteousness—know this! There are no human words to describe the wonders of the kingdom I have prepared as your new home.

My Son told you He was going to prepare a place for you. He will come back when you take your last breath. You will see the Light. You will never taste death. "Can a mother forget the baby at her breast and have no compassion on the child she has borne? Though she may forget, I will not forget you! See, I have engraved you on the palms of my hands; your walls are ever before me" (Isaiah 49:15-16).

My Prayer

Jesus, Lord, and Savior, I believe! (Acts 16:31). You are the eternal Word of God who brought forth the universe and all the living creatures within it. You called me into being and breathed into my lungs Your breath of life. You became flesh, entered time, and dwelt among us. You lived and died as love incarnate so that I might come to know You and, through You, greet my Father.

Gratitude brings me to kneel before You in worship. I am grateful that You made me, grateful for all the people whose love mirrored Your smile, grateful for all the experiences, both good and bad, that have shaped my soul and confirmed me in Your truth.

My life has never been a sufficient response to Your countless gifts. Forgive me. I could pray more, fast more, forgive more, share more, and love more. My sin is not so much what I have done, but what I have left undone. My sin is my lack of discipline, my laziness, my selfishness, my failure to empathize with the struggles and sufferings of others.

"For the Spirit God gave us does not make us timid, but gives us power, love, and self-discipline" (2 Timothy 1:7). Father, I have not fully embraced that power, love, or self-control, for I've allowed myself to be distracted and consumed with the pleasures of this world. I have sought the approval of others. I have eaten too much, drunk too much, and listlessly wasted time on the internet or television. There are a billion things I could have done to improve my mind or body that I ignored. I failed to seek out ways to make life better for others.

Come, Spirit, and renew my mind. Help me to discern Your will, what is good and acceptable and perfect (Romans 12:2). Father, I am Yours. Do with me as You choose, merciful Creator. Father, "For God so loved the world that he gave his one and only Son, that whoever believes in him shall not perish but have eternal life" (John 3:16). Be born within me once again, Spirit. Renew the bath of wind and fire. I believe; help my unbelief. Thy will be done.

I recommit myself to accepting Your divine will in all things. I give You the unknown as I embrace Your command to reject fear. I know that with Your Spirit, all things are possible, even my salvation, and that all things will work together for good. "I can do all things through him who gives me strength" (Philippians 4:13). Save me, Lord Jesus Christ.

"The grass withers and the flowers fall, but the word of God endures forever" (Isaiah 40:8). You, Jesus, are the Word made flesh, and I believe that You came to save me. Thank You for the gift of Your body and blood in the community of believers and in the gifts of Your Last Supper. You commanded, "Do this in memory of me." With faith in Your Word, I eat Your body and drink Your blood, You living in *me and me living in You (John 6:54-56). I strive to follow Your commandments (John 14:15).*

I pledge to love You, my God, with all my heart, with all my soul, with all my mind, and with all my strength. I strive to love my neighbor as myself (Mark 12:30-31). I believe in Your promise of resurrection and eternal life. I know that "Everyone who calls on the name of the Lord will be saved" (Romans 10:13). I accept You, Jesus, as my Lord and Savior. Save me, Lord Jesus, from eternal death. Save me from myself.

Heavenly Father, I will not live in fear though the night approaches. The Spirit confirms me in the truth. I walk each day in the shadow of Your wings. I stand in the light of Your teaching. I trust in Your will and surrender to Your plans. I know You will give me a future and a hope (Jeremiah 29:11). Fill me, Holy Spirit of Jesus, with hope, joy, and peace (Romans 15:13). The old order has passed away, so let the new one come. Praise to You, Lord Jesus Christ, who is, who was, and who is to come.

Spoken in the Spirit through Jesus, the Son, to the Father. Amen.

CHAPTER 14

BLESS THE LORD, MY SOUL

God is speaking to you. Listen!

The Jerusalem temple was built to offer Me blessing. Blessing is praise, but on a higher level. Blessing is reverential praise. The people were trying to extol My name, to give Me glory. They admired My work and respected Me. An entire cast of men, the Levites, was trained from birth to know My Word and to both shape and perform religious rites in the temple to offer Me blessing.

Melody was added to their blessing prayers, and from morning to night, 150 hymns floated with incense before My tabernacle on earth. Their songs echoed through the chambers of My kingdom in heaven and out to the farthest reaches of the universe.

"Praise the LORD, my soul; all my inmost being, praise his holy name. Praise the LORD, my soul, and forget not all his benefits—who forgives all your sins and heals all your diseases, who redeems your life from the pit and crowns you

with love and compassion, who satisfies your
desires with good things so that your youth
is renewed like the eagle's. The LORD works
righteousness and justice for all the oppressed. . .
. The LORD is compassionate and gracious, slow
to anger, abounding in love."

Psalm 103:1-6, 8

This song, like many, begins by blessing Me for personal benefits, then gives thanks for My mercy on all the people despite their sin. I know even the deepest depths of human depravity, but not even this can destroy My mercy. I know how fragile you are. Israel sang of My mercy, My forgiveness, My deep and abiding love. Their melodies reached up through the skies and moved the inhabitants of My heavenly kingdom to join in worship and mirror their hymns of praise.

I listened to the beating of their warm hearts as they sang out before Me. "Praise the LORD, my soul. LORD my God, you are great; you are clothed with splendor and majesty. The LORD wraps himself in light as with a garment; he stretches out the heavens like a tent and lays the beams of his upper chambers on their waters. He makes the clouds his chariot and rides on the wings of the wind. He makes winds his messengers, flames of fire his servants" (Psalm 104:1-4).

From the days the first temple was constructed to this day, these same hymns and many more have continued to pour into My heavenly kingdom from faith communities, simple homes, and monasteries throughout the world, and sometimes from your home.

Long ago, My Son's death tore open the temple veil that hid My Spirit from the people. A new age was about to begin.

A new temple will be built in which My Spirit would dwell. Jesus prophesied the coming of the Spirit, a Spirit the world can neither see nor know. "But you know him, for he lives with you and will be in you. I will not leave you orphans; I will come to you" (John 14:17-18). It is the Spirit within you that makes these blessing prayers possible. Without the Spirit, the mouth is silent, communal worship is poison, and the mind is consumed with the things of this world. The same reverential blessing of worship I accepted in the temple I now accept from your heart, My precious child. You are the temple of the Spirit. Your life is a hymn of blessing, an act of worship.

The Spirit, the Comforter, the Advocate within you brought you here to pray. I am listening. I welcome your words of blessing. I am attentive to your petitions. I reach out from heaven and touch your gratitude and embrace your thanksgiving as the clouds of incense rise before Me.

I accept your sacrifice of worship through Jesus, your intercessor. I will walk at your side. I choose each step of your journey now, My friend. I will return your worship by showering miracles upon you and those for whom you pray. Know this truth: I will never leave you or forsake you. My mercy endures forever.

My Prayer

Abba, Father, Creator, and King. I bless and extol Your holy name, for You have formed me from the clay of the earth, fashioned me within my mother's womb, breathed Your Spirit into me, and allowed me to know Your holy and glorious Son, Jesus. How wonderful this creation! I can see You now when I see Jesus. I can hear Your voice in Jesus. I can speak a new word now in the Spirit. Your Holy Spirit groans within me. I respond with a blessing to Your glory.

I give You blessing, Abba, for gifting me with faith. I could have lived my entire life without ever becoming aware of Your existence. I acknowledge You, God of Israel, Father of Jesus, as the one God, Creator. Many rise to eat, drink, and reproduce but never see Your face. How gracious You are to allow me to know that all I am or will ever be is a gift, and You are the giver.

Nothing is an accident in Your universe, but intentional, by design and purpose. You decided to set me here in this epoch and with these people as my brothers and sisters. You chose my unique experiences, and in that, You positioned each chisel strike against the stone, birthing my new heart. I am fearfully and wonderfully made. I bless You, Father. My words do not reach up to measure Your glory, for it is beyond my person to fathom the heights of Your holy Being. You designed my heart to contemplate Your wisdom. You fixed my path to shape my soul and lead me to contemplate Your love. I bless You, Father, that I exist!

I bless You, Creator, for fellowship within the body of Christ. I am not alone. I have companions on this ship, all made in Your image. They constantly remind me of Your love and lead me in Your Word and worship. Blessed are You, Father, for through Christ, You have given me a seat in Your orchestra that I might add my notes to the score. Experiencing the symphony of worship within the community of faith, I am swept up with the Spirit and feel peace, joy, and exaltation.

Blessed are You, Father, for the gift of people who love me and people for me to love. Wherever they are at this moment, whether in this world or the next, send Your Spirit upon them: my parents, spouse, children, grandchildren, family, and friends, relatives, and church community members. Heal them. Smile upon them. Offer them forgiveness and mercy. Give them abundant life. Give them faith in Jesus. You have designed relationships with others to amplify my relationship with You, triune God. I see You, God of love, when I see them.

I bless You in Your mighty deeds and Your laws. You make civil society possible. You have called us forth from among the animals that we might live and prosper, work together, and join together through worship. I appreciate the gifts You have showered upon my brothers and sisters everywhere and ask that as You have blessed me, I in turn might become a blessing to others. Bless the people of every country with freedom, safety, prosperity, and faith in Jesus. Restore sanity to civil society and guide the education of the young. Restore Your commandments to our common life especially those dealing with theft and murder. Gift all of us with a renewed sense of gratitude for the brave people that made so many sacrifices to build our culture and defend our country.

Crush the darkness of greed and pride that feed division and corrupt Your image within us and within me. Touch the hearts of gang members and those ruining our cities with retail theft, murder, and rape. Establish order, a sense of law, right and wrong, and end the moral corruption which is making daily living impossible. Bring both those who acknowledge You as God and those who do not believe in You to find common ground and work for a better world. Help our young to find a love for their country and give rebirth to a new sense of genuine patriotism. Help the human family to respect and care for the environment. Bridge the divisions we have forged, diminish the resentments and grudges of the past, lessen the heartache and pain we have sinfully fed through the centuries. Let all humanity become one harmonious family on earth to reflect the blessed and holy family of heaven, Father, Son, and Spirit. Thy kingdom come!

I bless You, Father, for being shepherd, protector, guide, doting parent, and defender. Your enemies abound. Those who reject Your path, mock Your honor, and craft lies to foster hate are relentless in their quest to take, to own, to strip others, and to enrich themselves. I am weak, and You are strength, Father. I am without a voice and cry out for Your hand of justice. I will follow where You lead and bear axe, pick, and shovel to build Your kingdom. I trust Your faithfulness, walk in Your way, and obey Your every command. I lie down in Your peace. All blessing and praise to You, Father. Make us all feel safe within our homes and as we walk the streets.

I bless You, Lord Yahweh, Elohim, for You hear my prayer. When I speak, You show me favor and listen. You never mock my words or count my plea as worthless. You hear my cries for help, and I am privileged to stand within Your temple and offer worship. Make straight my way and show me the path I must follow that leads to You. Surround me with Your favor like a shield and silence my enemies. Spirit of God, groan out and echo my sighs that each prayer reach the Father's ears and pierce His heart. You see my weeping and take up my plea. I celebrate You who deign to listen to my worship song.

"I will give thanks to you, LORD, with all my heart; I will tell of all your wonderful deeds. I will be glad and rejoice in you; I will sing the praises of your name, O Most High" (Psalm 9:1-2).

Spoken in the Spirit through Jesus, the Son, to the Father. Amen.

CHAPTER 15

LIGHT OF THE WORLD

God is speaking to you. Listen!

"You are the light of the world. A town built on a hill cannot be hidden. Neither do people light a lamp and put it under a bowl. Instead, they put it on its stand, and it gives light to everyone in the house. In the same way, let your light shine before others, that they may see your good deeds and glorify your Father in heaven."

Matthew 5:14-16

J esus did not say you *might be* the light of the world. He did not say you *could be* the light of the world. He said you are the light of the world. This is not just an aspiration; it is a declaration of who you are in Christ. I created you to be a reflection of My light, to shine forth in the darkness, to be a beacon of hope and truth in a world often overshadowed by despair and falsehood. Your light is not just for yourself; it is for the world around you.

Light has a unique quality. It dispels darkness without struggle or effort. When light enters a room, darkness flees. Darkness has no power over light. This is the truth I want you to hold onto: The light within you, the light that comes from My Spirit, is more powerful than any darkness you will face. It is not your light alone but My light shining through you. You are a vessel of My presence, a carrier of My divine love and truth.

Think about the ways in which light serves. It illuminates the path, guiding those who are lost or confused. It brings warmth, comforting those who are cold or afraid. It reveals truth, exposing what is hidden in shadows. It is a source of life, enabling growth and flourishing. This is what you are called to do in the world. You are to guide, to comfort, to reveal, and to bring life. Your light is meant to be shared, not hidden.

"You are the light of the world. A town built on a hill cannot be hidden" (Matthew 5:14). Your life, your actions, your words—they are all seen by others. You may think you can hide your faith, that you can live in secret devotion, but the truth is, your light will shine, whether you want it to or not. People are watching you, noticing how you live, how you respond to challenges, how you treat others. Your life is a testimony to My presence within you.

The question is not whether your light will shine but how brightly it will shine. Will it be a flicker, barely visible in the darkness? Or will it be a blazing torch, guiding others to Me? The more you allow My Spirit to work in you, the brighter your light will become. The more you trust in Me, the more you will reflect My love and truth. The more you surrender to My will, the more you will become a beacon of hope to those around you.

But remember this: Light is not something you generate on your own. You do not have to strive to create it. The light you carry is a gift from Me. It is My presence within you, My Spirit alive and active in your life. Your role is to keep that light burning, to tend to it with care, to protect it from anything that would seek to extinguish it.

One way to keep your light shining brightly is through worship. Worship is like oil to the lamp, fueling the flame of your faith. When you worship Me, you are reminded of who I am and who you are in Me. Worship draws you closer to My heart, aligning your spirit with Mine. It fills you with My presence, strengthens your faith, and renews your commitment to live as a light in the world.

Another way to keep your light burning is through love. Love is the essence of My light. When you love others, you are reflecting My nature, revealing My character. Love is much more than a simple emotion; it is a choice, a decision to put others before yourself, to serve, to forgive, to show kindness and compassion. When you love, you are shining My light into the lives of those around you.

Finally, stay connected to My Word. My Word is a lamp for your feet and a light on your path (Psalm 119:105). It guides you, instructs you, and keeps you grounded in truth. When you immerse yourself in My Word, you are filling your life with light, equipping yourself to shine brightly in a dark world.

My Prayer

Heavenly Father, I thank You for the light You have placed within me. I recognize that this light is not my own but a reflection of Your divine presence. Help me to be a faithful steward of this light, to shine brightly in a world that so desperately needs hope, truth, and love.

Jesus, You said that I am the light of the world. I accept this calling and ask for Your help to live it out each day. When I am tempted to hide my light, remind me of Your words. When I am afraid to let my light shine, give me courage. When I feel weak and inadequate, fill me with Your strength.

Holy Spirit, empower me to be a beacon of hope and truth. Guide my steps so that I may walk in Your light. Fill my heart with Your love so that I may reflect it to those around me. Keep me grounded in Your Word so that I may stand firm in the truth.

Lord, let my light shine before others in such a way that they may see my good deeds and glorify You, my Father in heaven. May my life be a testimony to Your goodness, Your grace, and Your love. May others be drawn to You through the light You have placed within me.

Thank You, Father, for the privilege of being a light in the world. Help me to live each day in a way that honors You and brings glory to Your name. I trust in Your promise that as I shine Your light, You will be with me, guiding me, and giving me strength.

Spoken in the Spirit through Jesus, the Son, to the Father. Amen.

CHAPTER 16

BE STILL AND KNOW

God is speaking to you. Listen!

---

*"Be still, and know that I am God; I will be
exalted among the nations, I will be exalted in the
earth."*

Psalm 46:10

I n the midst of your busy life, I call you to stillness. The
world around you is filled with noise—voices clamoring
for your attention, demands pulling you in every direction, responsibilities that weigh heavily on your shoulders.
Yet in the middle of it all, I invite you to pause, to be still,
to recognize My presence. It is in this stillness that you will
come to truly know Me.

When I ask you to be still, I am not merely talking about
physical stillness, though that is part of it. I am asking you to
quiet your mind, to set aside your worries, to let go of your
striving. I am asking you to stop trying to control everything,
to stop wrestling with problems that are beyond your ability

119

to solve. I am inviting you to trust Me, to rest in My sovereignty, to acknowledge that I am God.

Stillness is a posture of the heart. It is a place of surrender, where you lay down your burdens and open your heart to receive My peace. It is a place where you stop striving, stop trying to earn My favor, and simply rest in My love. It is a place of deep trust, where you release your anxieties and fears into My hands, knowing that I am in control.

In the stillness, you will find Me. I am not far from you. I am closer than your breath, nearer than your next heartbeat. But you must be still to sense My presence, to hear My voice. It is in the quiet moments that I speak to your heart, that I whisper My love to you, that I guide you with My wisdom.

You live in a world that values activity and achievement, that measures success by how much you do and how much you produce. But My kingdom is different. In My kingdom, being still is an act of faith. It is a declaration that you trust Me more than you trust your own efforts. It is an acknowledgment that I am the source of all good things, that apart from Me you can do nothing (John 15:5).

When you are still, you are reminded of My greatness. You are reminded that I am the Creator of the heavens and the earth, that I hold the universe in My hands. You are reminded that I am the One who sustains all things, who brings order out of chaos, who calms the storm with a word. You are reminded that I am God, and there is no other.

Being still is not easy. It requires discipline, especially in a world that is constantly on the move. It requires intentionality, a decision to step away from the busyness and enter into My presence. But when you do, you will find rest for your soul. You will find peace that surpasses understanding. You will find strength for the journey ahead.

"Be still, and know that I am God." This is not just a suggestion; it is a command. I am calling you to a deeper relationship with Me, one that is not based on what you do, but on who I am. I am calling you to trust Me in the midst of uncertainty, to rest in My promises, to find your security in My unchanging nature.

In the stillness, you will come to know Me in ways you have never known before. You will see My hand at work in your life, guiding you, protecting you, providing for you. You will hear My voice more clearly, speaking words of comfort, direction, and encouragement. You will experience My presence in a profound way, filling you with joy, peace, and love.

So, come to Me. Be still. Lay down your burdens. Stop striving. Rest in My love. Know that I am God, and that I am with you always.

My Prayer

Father, I come before You now, seeking the stillness that only You can provide. In the midst of my busy life, I long to experience Your presence in a deeper way. I ask that You help me to quiet my mind, to set aside my worries, and to focus on You.

Jesus, I trust in Your words, "Come to me, all you who are weary and burdened, and I will give you rest" (Matthew 11:28). I bring my burdens to You now, laying them at Your feet. I surrender my anxieties, my fears, and my need to control. I choose to be still, to rest in Your love, and to trust in Your sovereign plan for my life.

Holy Spirit, help me to cultivate a posture of stillness in my heart. Remind me to pause throughout my day, to take moments to be still and to acknowledge Your presence. Guide me in Your truth, and lead me in the way everlasting.

Father, in the stillness, I want to know You more. I want to experience Your peace, to hear Your voice, and to feel Your love. I ask that You reveal Yourself to me in new and powerful ways as I seek to be still before You.

Thank You, Lord, for the gift of stillness. Thank You for the invitation to rest in Your presence and to trust in Your goodness. I choose to embrace this gift, to be still, and to know that You are God.

Spoken in the Spirit through Jesus, the Son, to the Father. Amen.

CHAPTER 17

SURRENDER INTO JESUS' ARMS

God is speaking to you. Listen!

---

*"For whoever wants to save their life will lose it,
but whoever loses their life for me will find it."*

Matthew 16:25

Who does the saving—you or Me? The name Jesus means "God saves." Not you! If it is I who save, then you need to give Me your life. Right? You need to surrender your life into My care. It is an act of trust. I want it all—no holding back, no buts. Trust Me with your past, present, and future. "Submit yourselves, then, to God. Resist the devil, and he will flee from you" (James 4:7). I will have no other gods before Me.

When a soldier surrenders, they recognize that their efforts are powerless, ineffective, and empty. Leadership has failed. A universal sign of surrender is raised, empty hands. No weapon. No hammer and nails. No food. No bottle of water.

No plans. An infant's hands are born this way. Surrender involves a willingness to accept a new voice as commander, leader, protector, guardian, benefactor, father, and mother. Surrender is a total, absolute giving over of oneself into the hands of another.

Surrender begins with an honest appraisal of one's life that says, "I cannot do this on my own. I need help." It is a lesson in both humility and vulnerability. Recall the story Jesus told about the father who brought his possessed son and laid him at the Lord's feet. At this point, the father had tried everything and found his efforts fruitless.

His humble submission made him vulnerable. There was no guarantee as to how Jesus would respond. The act of surrender is in itself imperfect. "I do believe; help me overcome my unbelief!" (Mark 9:24). But Jesus did not tell the man to return after the man left. Trust has the final word. Imagine dropping a child at another's feet and trusting a perfect stranger with their life? Faith is a leap from a precipice without the absolute guarantee that someone will be there to catch you. You leap anyway. It is perfect yet imperfect at the same time. The leap is in itself your statement that I AM love, and whether I catch you or not, you belong to Me from the moment you take that first leap.

Surrendering to Jesus is a leap into a new way of living in the world. The self-reliant life, where you have to come up with every answer and solution, is surrendered to the Spirit. You trust that My Spirit within your heart will guide your steps. My written voice in Scripture and the voice of the Spirit within your heart will direct your path. Your hands stretch out, and you give yourself to a way of life that embraces the cross. Always remember that there is no Christianity without the cross.

Jesus served as an example to you of the act of surrendering in Gethsemane when He prayed, "Your will be done" (Matthew 6:9). He completed the act on the cross when He gave over His spirit to Me, the Father (Luke 23:46).

"Those who belong to Christ Jesus have crucified the flesh with its passions and desires. Since we live by the Spirit, let us keep in step with the Spirit" (Galatians 5:24-25). Paul said, "I have been crucified with Christ and I no longer live, but Christ lives in me" (Galatians 2:20). Open hands and raised arms render you defenseless, vulnerable. Jesus modeled this leap into the unknown from the cross. "Father, into your hands I commit my spirit" (Luke 23:46).

Surrender must always be chosen, never forced. Without the free will gift of yourself, there can be no sacrifice, and therefore, no glory. "For many are invited, but few are chosen" (Matthew 22:14).

My Prayer

Father, Creator, Almighty God, Elohim, please hear me!

How could I have journeyed so long without You? Why was I deaf to the sound of Your call? Given this world of wonder and goodness, how could it come to be but through You? How blind I have been not to have fixed my mind on the blessings You profusely poured into my life and returned to kneel before You in thanksgiving. Your fingerprints are everywhere. I was preoccupied with trivia and the inconsequential, distracted from what is real, good, true, and beautiful.

It was not only the multitude of gifts You poured into my life but also suffering that brings me to Your feet. In a way, I'm actually grateful for the mess I'm experiencing right now, for it woke me up to Your presence, Lord. Misery canceled my arrogance and turned my head. Misfortune made me humble. As I am brought low, I affirm that You are here with me. You have always been here.

"'For I know the plans I have for you,' declares the LORD, 'plans to prosper you and not to harm you, plans to give you hope and a future. Then you will call on me and come and pray to me, and I will listen to you. You will seek me and find me when you seek me with all your heart. I will be found by you,' declares the LORD" (Jeremiah 29:11-14). You have all my heart now, Father.

I am finally ready to listen to Your voice, Lord, but it isn't easy. I'm not sure sometimes if I'm understanding what You want me to do or say. I try to ponder what I read in Scripture, but the words sometimes seem to be floating down to me through water, and I'm at the bottom of a lake trying to catch them. I feel like my brain is working too slowly to lay hold of the meaning. Are other people that much smarter than I am? I won't give up, though, Lord. You just may have to repeat Yourself several times, like Your call to young Samuel in the temple.

Over and over, You summoned Samuel until finally, it all clicked in his mind, and he recognized Your voice. Samuel said, "Speak, for your servant is listening" (1 Samuel 3:10). The more I come to know You, Father, the more I will understand my place and purpose. I understand and accept the fact that bad things happen to everyone.

Lord, I commit myself to keep Your commandments. I will rejoice in hope, anticipate others by showing honor and favor, be fervent in spirit, endure affliction, and persevere in prayer. I will bless those who persecute me, rejoice with those who rejoice, and weep with those who weep. I will not repay evil for evil but seek reconciliation, forgiving every fault. I will love my enemies. I will live in peace with everyone.

To love like You, Jesus, I know I must die to myself and live in You. I accept You, Jesus Christ, as my Lord and Savior. I trust You with my life. I surrender myself, body and soul, to Your love and care. Let it be done to me according to Your Word. (Romans 12:11-15)

Why surrender? First, Father, You made the vessel, so You own it. My life belongs to You, and I exist for Your pleasure. "Do you not know that your bodies are temples of the Holy Spirit, who is in you, whom you have received from God? You are not your own; you were bought at a price" (1 Corinthians 6:19-20).

Second, as my Creator, You have my best interests in mind. You have a plan and a purpose for my life (Jeremiah 29:11). Third, You love me enough to allow Jesus to die for me on the cross. It is Jesus who, through His death, offers me back to You (John 17:6-26). Fourth, I invite You to come and take what I recognize is Yours—my body and soul, my mind and heart (Psalm 37:5).

So, Father, now that You've moved in, I won't complain that You are ripping up the floors and tearing down walls. I expect my life to see some major remodeling. "Yet you, LORD, are our Father. We are the clay; you are the potter; we are all the work of your hand" (Isaiah 64:8). "I am the Lord's servant . . . May your word to me be fulfilled" (Luke 1:38).

Father, "You have searched me, LORD, and you know me. . . . Where can I go from your Spirit? Where can I flee from your presence? . . . For you created my inmost being; you knit me together in my mother's womb. I praise you because I am fearfully and wonderfully made; your works are wonderful, I know that full well" (Psalm 139:1,7,13-14).

To You and to You alone, Father, I give honor and glory. You called me even though I knew You not. Your favor has shone down upon me. There is no other God besides You, the one God. I am the marble, and You are the sculptor. To You, Father, I bend my knee and bow my head. Father, You said, "Turn to me and be saved, all you ends of the earth; for I am God, and there is no other" (Isaiah 45:22).

I proclaim You, Jesus, my Lord and God. I stand in faith that You have died and risen to redeem my life from the grave. I know my vindicator lives and that one day I will stand upon the dust and see You. I myself shall see You face to face, Jesus, my King, after my spirit leaves this body and rises by Your power. With my own eyes, I shall behold You. From my flesh, I shall see God. That is Your promise to me, Father. My inmost being is consumed with longing. (Job 19)

Spoken in the Spirit through Jesus, the Son, to the Father. Amen.

CHAPTER 18

JESUS PROCLAIMS LIBERTY TO CAPTIVES

God is speaking to you. Listen!

My first thirty-three years on earth were preparation for My public ministry, which began the day I entered the synagogue in My hometown. I retrieved the scroll of Isaiah and went to the pulpit. I found the prophecy that announced My coming. I was not just speaking to those seated before Me. I had you in My mind. I could see you even though you had not yet taken your first breath. I was speaking to you on that day in the synagogue. This is personal.

> *"The Spirit of the Lord is on me, because he has anointed me to proclaim good news to the poor. He has sent me to proclaim freedom for the prisoners and recovery of sight for the blind, to set the oppressed free, to proclaim the year of the Lord's favor."*
>
> Luke 4:18-19

Every word was spoken with you in mind, but right now, I'd like to talk about two phrases: "proclaim freedom for the prisoners" and "set the oppressed free." You are both captive and oppressed. You are not free. You are bound and chained.

How is this true? In many ways! You are bound by the guilt of thinking yourself a failure for the mistakes of your adult children. You are bound by the memory of words spoken that cannot be taken back. You are bound by the trauma of suicide, betrayal, abortion, bound by a broken heart, shattered dreams, and grief. Should I go on? You are a slave to alcohol, drugs, overeating, a sexual habit, bound by anxiety, depression, painkillers, or by your own sense of worthlessness.

Huddled in the dark prison of your heart, you have slowly drifted into silence. Why should your prayers be constant if there is no God to hear your plea? All the bad things that happened beat you down, and you began to change. Your laughter became false; your words empty. Hope vanquished. You thought, *This is who I am and will always be. There is no way out.*

I am your Friend, your Savior. I am speaking directly to you now. Do you hear Me? Do those two words I mentioned ring true—captive and oppressed? Do they sound personal? This is the time to break the chains that hold you captive. I send My angels to you just as I sent them to Peter and Paul in prison. I command the chains to break. Get up and follow the angels into the light. "Forget the former things; do not dwell on the past. See, I am doing a new thing! Now it springs up; do you not perceive it? I am making a way in the wilderness and streams in the wasteland" (Isaiah 43:18-19).

My children, please hear Me. I can't bear your suffering any longer. You might understand My message today if you listen in as I direct My words now to one particular individual who is reading this. I turn My gaze on the chains that hold her bound. She buried her teenage daughter after suicide. This mother's grief is unspeakable, her torment unending. She fears her daughter might be in hell. She blames herself for a thousand attempts to help her daughter that failed. She wonders if she had behaved differently, said something, done something, had fewer rules, or taken her daughter to different doctors, her daughter might still be alive. Listen in now as I speak to this woman.

You have buried a child. A sword like no other has pierced your heart. You love your daughter. I love her more. You would give your life, your soul, to see your daughter happy and alive. I already did that for her and for you. I came and gave the world My body and My soul. I died through Jesus, My only Son, that you and your precious child might have life. Your daughter is with Me. She lives. Can't you feel her spirit? Her love for you, her mother, still lives. Love does not die. Your daughter looks down from heaven and sees your pain. She has been praying for you! I was speaking to her and to you when I promised never to leave you or forsake you (Deuteronomy 31:6).

Your sadness breaks My heart. Your prison of grief is not My design. You must allow the chains to fall. You must stand up of your own volition. Will it! Let these memories of your daughter's death receive My light. Stop the blaming. The past is gone. Your daughter lives. I am the resurrection. Stand and believe in My divine mercy. Mercy is a gift given when it is not deserved. Am I not free to do what I please? I am the Lord God, and there is no other. I can forgive the unforgivable. Mercy, by definition, gives forgiveness and not justice.

I did not plan your daughter's manner of death. I cried through the tears of Jesus. Jesus wept not just before the grave of Lazarus, but in that moment, He wept with you. We were not distant or strangers to your daughter's suffering, her self-hatred, the depth of her depression, the nightmare of her addictions. She made poor choices. She was selfish and narcissistic. Your daughter was starved for love, and no matter who offered it, including Me, she could not escape the prison she had fashioned within her mind. Jesus wept with you, My child. He knew your daughter's pain, and He knows yours.

I am love, and now that your daughter and My daughter is free of her body, I fill her soul. Your daughter's glorified and restored body will rise again on the last day, together with yours. Nothing shall be denied her in the afterlife. I would not let one moment of pain erase your daughter's love, her hunger for life, memories of her first word, her first smile, her unsteady venture at walking. She was Mine before she was yours. It is not My nature to be cruel, and I am not a sadist taking pleasure in pain. I would not, could not, make her suffer more once she abandoned earth. I have healed and restored your daughter. Unplanned, she fell into My arms, and I will keep her safe until you are called forth to meet her.

Embrace the love of Jesus and let the chains of your bondage fall away. The Spirit will confirm My words today to be true. Test your heart now. The sin that binds you, mother, is not something your daughter has done, but what you have left undiscovered—My divine mercy and My love. I am love. Your daughter lives.

"For we know that our old self was crucified with Him so that the body ruled by sin might be done away with, that we should no longer be slaves to sin. . . . In the same way, count yourselves dead to sin but alive to God in Christ Jesus" (Romans 6:6, 11).

"The Spirit you received does not make you slaves, so that you live in fear again; rather, the Spirit you received brought about your adoption to sonship. And by him we cry, 'Abba, Father'" (Romans 8:15). Child, hear Me now and believe in Me. I will always love you. Trust Me. When you see Jesus, you see Me.

It was in My name that Jesus entered the synagogue and chose the scroll of Isaiah's prophecies. Our words in Scripture were alive then, and they remain living at this moment. I proclaim liberty to you who are captive and oppressed. Be free of your bad marriage, your addictions, your self-hatred, your financial worries, your health concerns, your unanswered prayers, your expired dreams, your constant worry. Leave the past that binds you and come live in My light (1 John 1:7).

My Prayer

Abba, Father, You are truly with me. I feel the Holy Spirit. Such a wonderful gift! I don't know whether I should cry or laugh, scream or remain silent. How long have I been a captive and not known it? How long have these chains bound my heart and tormented my mind? Through the Word of Jesus, I know my Helper, the Holy Spirit, is teaching me things through these prayers (John 14:26). I am seeing now the truth of Your love, Your faithfulness, Your mercy! How could I not have seen this before?

I submit myself to Your embrace. I will love You with all my heart and with all my soul and with all my strength and with all my mind (Luke 10:27). I will not allow my bad experiences or painful memories to bind me in self-torment or self-pity. You came to set me free from this darkness. You came to help me bury this old self, to leave it in the grave, and to rise to a new life—a life defined by Your words, a life led by You, a life ablaze with energy, a life that affirms Your constant love and care. You are the Lord God who brings me out of the land of slavery so I will not be bound to guilt or alcohol or broken promises or nightmares from the past.

I had stopped groaning, crying out in prayer because being miserable became my new normal. I wallowed in self-pity and thought of myself as a victim of circumstance. I had forgotten what true peace might be like. My prison became my normal. My spirit was numb. My mouth sewn shut. But now I hear Your call, Jesus. I feel Your presence and know I am loved. My past is over. You have spoken over me and declared me worthy.

Jesus, You set me free from all that binds me. You enter time and history and orchestrate my awakening. You see my way to the cross and move to my side just like Simon slipped in beside You to help carry the cross. It is Your Word that breaks my chains and moves the stone from my tomb. You said, "Everything is possible for one who believes" (Mark 9:23). I do believe; help my unbelief!

"You deaf and mute spirit, I command you, come out of him and never enter him again" (Mark 9:25). Free me from the liar, Jesus. Silence his voice. Purify me and open my mouth to proclaim Your glory. Take all my sins away. Set me free. Unbind all that fetters my spirit that I might sing Your praise. Heal my eyes that I can see Your miracles. Make me mindful of Your wonders. Touch my lips with Your burning coal and mark them with Your brand. May all I see and say please You and bring You glory. You, God of Israel, are ready to pardon, gracious, and merciful, slow to anger, and of great kindness. (Nehemiah 9:17)

Christ, You have made me free. I stand in liberty and will not go back to bondage. I claim the Spirit of Jesus. Help me to live in love. I will be patient and kind. I will never be rude or seek my own interests or be quick-tempered. I will not brood over my injuries but pray for my persecutors. I will not feed on the negative, the wrongdoing, but will search for the good in every person and situation. I will search for the good even in myself and proclaim Your glory, Father. "God saw all that he had made, and it was very good" (Genesis 1:31). God made me! And I am good!

In the name of the Father, and of the Son, and of the Holy Spirit.

Spoken in the Spirit through Jesus, the Son, to the Father. Amen.

CHAPTER 19

FIVE WAYS OF PRAYER

God is speaking to you. Listen!

I heard you knock. I open the door. Come in. This is the way it should be with friends. You just felt like you didn't want to be alone. You chose Me. Casual. No rush. Content just to be here. We don't need to speak or do anything in particular. This is how it is with family. We don't have to entertain each other. Most often, we are both silent, but sometimes one of us will speak softly. This is the heart of all prayer. Draw near.

"Come near to God and he will come near to you. Wash your hands, you sinners, and purify your hearts, you double-minded. Grieve, mourn, and wail. Change your laughter to mourning and your joy to gloom. Humble yourselves before the Lord, and he will lift you up."

James 4:8-10

Many people think of lists when they think of prayer, as if they were going to a market and didn't want to get home to find out they forgot the milk. Johnnie is depressed. Margaret has cancer. Jennie is having problems in her marriage. Conflict in the Middle East. Politics. Hurricanes. Final exams. Bob is still drinking. Cindy is eating herself to death. They might as well just hand Me the list at the door and go away. They never really want to come in and rest at My side anyway. It's like Door Dash. They get fidgety toward the bottom of the list. Their minds wander somewhere else. They might as well be on their way. Don't get Me wrong. I welcome your lists and intercessory prayers because they tell Me you actually care about other people's struggles. I am always happy to help out. This way of prayer is ***intercession***.

"Carry each other's burdens, and in this way, you will fulfill the law of Christ" (Galatians 6:2). "Pray for each other" (James 5:16).

But here you are. No lists today? You just came to be with Me, so draw near, My friend. Sit by My side. This is the prayer with no words. Part of your coming was to remember who I am and what I did. You like My story and enter it every time you open Scripture. Little by little over the years, our closeness has changed you. You've become more and more like Me without any conscious choice to do so. Parents tell their children to choose their friends wisely because they know just being around someone will change who they become. My words have become part of who you are (John 15:7). This way of prayer is called ***contemplation***.

You like Me! You like being with Me. You are proud just to be thought worthy to enter My home and sit by My side. Part of you can't figure out why I chose you to be My friend. Others might be proud to tell everyone Oprah invited them over for a glass of wine or Tiger Woods asked them to play some golf, but you are elated to be with Me. You choose to be with Me as much as possible. You are grateful.

You are grateful to know Me, grateful for who I am, grateful for what I do in the world. My Holy Spirit wells up from deep within your soul in adoration and reverence. The faith I gave now returns to Me through you. You are lifting yourself up to Me in sacrifice in these moments, giving yourself over to My divine will. You were made to know, love, and serve Me, and in these moments, you are doing all three.

You want to sing out your joy, and sometimes you do exactly that. You feel this tremendous impulse to gather with other believers so that together you may all offer your prayers to Me through Jesus. This gathering is a moment of communal self-sacrifice. This form of prayer is **worship**.

I notice that you keep going back to how you were before I came into your life. In your life before Me, you were not exactly sure what, if anything, was missing; only that something was amiss, tilted, not right. On one level, you sensed something was wrong, but on the other hand, you were quite certain everything was as it should be. Not one ounce of guilt. The fact is, you were quite proud of yourself back then.

But you have changed. You see more clearly now. You wonder who that person was that you used to be. The past you seems a stranger drifting further away from shore. When we first met, you needed to explain in great detail all your choices and how those choices brought suffering into your life and the lives of others. You wanted to make sure I knew who I was getting into a relationship with. This confession of sin is part of owning and then burying it. Your past exists no more. You are the only one who keeps taking the past from the shelf to reexamine its contours. It is time to leave the past alone. It's just you and Me in the here and now. Peace. Forgiveness. Forgive one another. Forgive yourself. This type of prayer is **confession** or **reconciliation**.

Our friendship has grown into something more. The Spirit within you has connected you to others similarly blessed and gifted. Together you have become the body of Christ. Jesus is living in you and you in Him and He in Me. We, a Trinity of persons, are one with you. This is the highest form of prayer possible for human beings.

You are with Me no longer just on a spiritual level but on a physical level. Creation itself has been altered in communion. We share the same heartbeat. This prayer is **communion**, where you are one in Us—Jesus, the Father and Holy Spirit and through us, one with each other. (John 14:15-31)

These five ways of prayer constitute the language of love. Five openings to the waters of life. These waters enter your bloodstream and change who you are in the world. "The Spirit and the bride say, 'Come!' And let the one who hears say, 'Come!' Let the one who is thirsty come; and let the one who wishes take the free gift of the water of life" (Revelation 22:17).

My Prayer

Father, Jesus, Holy Spirit! Praise! Glory! Blessing! Adoration! Worship!

You looked on what I was and forgave me. You took all of me: my mistakes, my anger and rage, my laziness and indulgence, my heart of stone, apathy, mean spirit, cruel words, revenge, urge to kill and destroy, as well as my kindness, sacrifice, mercy, charity, and love. You took it all, the bad and the good, and without denying anything of what I was, transformed the whole of who I was into who I am, someone new. I was reborn in the Spirit. You took my sin and made grace. You stepped into the abyss and called forth Your creation. Glory and blessing be unto You, my Lord and my God.

I do not know what to pray for as I ought, so in Your mercy, You sent the Spirit. The Spirit intercedes for me and for the whole community of believers and, with wordless groans, painfully lifts up prayers for Thy will to be done on earth and in heaven. (Romans 8:26)

Help me, Spirit of God! Help me to continually forgive the petty grievances I clutch as You have forgiven me. Empower me to let go. Make of me an instrument of peace, a witness to Your gentleness, and help me to reflect Your kindness and mercy. Lord, teach me to be humble and patient. Make me kind and tolerant. Sacred heart of Jesus, pour Your blood on me. Cover me with Your hand and shield me from the enemy. Let my life become a prayer to live to Your glory.

Spirit of God, consume me as I consume the Bread of Life and Your Holy Word in Scripture. Make me one with You and with my brothers and sisters everywhere. Take this creature of flesh and blood and glorify my spirit that I might become Your body. Bless me with Your Holy Communion, as unworthy as I am. This communion will place me on the cross with Jesus. Being one in Christ with other Christians will be my final test before I enter the heavenly kingdom.

Dwell within me, Holy Spirit, and make me one with the Father and Jesus. I cast away all prejudice and racism from my heart. I cast away privilege and pride. I renounce sin. I stand side by side, shoulder to shoulder, equal to my brothers and sisters. I confess myself to be no more than a sinner in need of the Savior. I commit myself to walk the way of Christ, to work for justice, and to build a kingdom of love. I commit myself to look for the good in others and to bring people together. Make me one with all my brothers and sisters in the body of Christ.

Glory to You, Father, Son, and Spirit, who is now, forever has been, and will always be.

Spoken in the Spirit through Jesus, the Son, to the Father. Amen.

CHAPTER 20

THE MONEY PROBLEM

God is speaking to you. Listen!

"Keep your lives free from the love of money and be content with what you have, because God has said, 'Never will I leave you; never will I forsake you.' So we say with confidence, 'The Lord is my helper; I will not be afraid. What can mere mortals do to me?'"

Hebrews 13:5-6

"Their destiny is destruction, their god is their stomach, and their glory is in their shame. Their mind is set on earthly things."

Philippians 3:19

It is the Lord God who speaks: "I know how troubled you are about your finances. Do not be discouraged." The Bible passages I just quoted are not to be understood as a condemnation of your anxiety over money. A man told his wife not to cry when their child died. How can the mother not cry over her child's grave? And so, with your concern over paying your bills. How could you not worry? I made you. I gave you feelings for a reason. I know you cannot turn your feelings on and off with a switch.

Grief, anxiety, fear, depression, anger, even sexual urges are part of My creation. All your feelings, even pain, are gifts designed for your well-being. You are not a bad person for having feelings that are unpleasant. You are not a faithless person because you worry about money. You have children to feed, bills to pay, a life to build, loved ones to protect.

There would be something wrong with you if you were incapable of worrying about money. Sociopaths don't worry. They are the corruption of My design. You are not. You worry over many things. Worry can serve you. You worry about cancer and stop smoking. You worry about accidents and slow down while driving. You worry about being assaulted and avoid dangerous places. You worry over money and take care what you spend. Worry over money becomes an issue only when it no longer serves your well-being or displaces My place in your heart.

How much is enough? This is where the cancer starts. One cell. One word: enough. You need enough to provide food, shelter, health, entertainment, beauty, and charity for yourself and your family. Being blessed with having all your basic needs met should usher in a moment to pause and reflect on how you might become a blessing to others.

Having a car that is paid for and money to spare is when you ask if others have transportation, not how to buy a newer car simply because you have sufficient funds.

Having a home that you can adequately finance is not when you begin looking for a more expensive home, but when you ask if others have shelter. Having food on your table is not when you look for a fine restaurant, but when you ask if others can feed their children. Jesus was clear in that the measure of your care and concern for others will be the measure used for your eternal salvation. At the last judgment, He will proclaim, "Truly I tell you, whatever you did for one of the least of these brothers and sisters of mine, you did for me" (Matthew 25:40).

"Philip said, 'Lord, show us the Father and that will be enough for us'" (John 14:8). Your faith in Jesus is the single most valuable gift you will ever receive. "For it is by grace you have been saved, through faith—and this is not for yourselves, it is the gift of God—not by works, so that no one can boast. For we are God's handiwork, created in Christ Jesus to do good works, which God prepared in advance for us to do" (Ephesians 2:8-10).

You were born and planted where and when you were for a reason, and that reason is not to enrich yourself, but to build My kingdom. Your faith in Jesus will show you the way to do that. You are My handiwork, made to carry out the good works I will show you. You were not made simply to enrich yourself. An animal thinks only of its own needs. You have a greater purpose. You are made in My image and likeness.

Having faith means you live with confidence that I am always with you and will provide for your essential needs. Trust Me with tomorrow. "Therefore I tell you, do not worry about your life, what you will eat or drink; or about your body, what you will wear . . . Do not worry about tomorrow, for tomorrow will worry about itself. Each day has enough trouble of its own" (Matthew 6:25, 34).

Having faith means you surrender yourself into My care and trust Me to be a good shepherd. If you are anxious every day, perhaps there is a need to pause and ask yourself first if your anxiety has foundation and second if you are living with trust in My providence.

"You shall have no other gods before me" (Exodus 20:3). Some have given the throne of their hearts to the love of money. They are consumed with having more. Serving Me, glorifying My name, and giving themselves over in self-sacrifice to their brothers and sisters is a struggle for them.

Often, these same people have not found their way into fellowship with other Christians. They feel an emptiness inside they try to fill with adulation, material objects, power, and position in society. They are miserable, isolated creatures who do not know how unhappy they are. They never feel they have enough or are enough. "From everyone who has been given much, much will be demanded; and from the one who has been entrusted with much, much more will be asked" (Luke 12:48).

My children need to examine and reexamine the relationship they have with the things of this world to see if they are remaining focused on the kingdom.

"Do not wear yourself out to get rich; do not trust your own cleverness. Cast but a glance at riches, and they are gone, for they will surely sprout wings and fly off to the sky like an eagle" (Proverbs 23:4-5). "Is not life more than food, and the body more than clothes?" (Matthew 6:25). "Faith by itself, if it is not accompanied by action, is dead" (James 2:17).

All gifts demand a response. Sometimes a simple "Thank you" is sufficient, but gifts from the living God demand more than a word of thanks. My blessings demand nothing less than sacrificial worship. Take a measure of your gifts and bring them to Me at the altar. Or should you offer these same gifts to your brother or sister, be assured you are offering them to Me.

"If anyone has material possessions and sees a brother or sister in need but has no pity on them, how can the love of God be in that person? Dear children, let us not love with words or speech but with actions and in truth."
1 John 3:17-18

"You will be enriched in every way so that you can be generous on every occasion, and through us your generosity will result in thanksgiving to God" (2 Corinthians 9:11). When you touch the lives of the poor, you are offering a sacrifice of worship, and I am glorified in you.

"For we brought nothing into the world, and we can take nothing out of it. For the love of money is a root of all kinds of evil. Some people, eager for money, have wandered from the faith and pierced themselves with many griefs. But you, man of God, flee from all this, and pursue righteousness, godliness, faith, love, endurance, and gentleness. Fight the good fight of the faith. Take hold of the eternal life to which you were called when you made your good confession in the presence of many witnesses" (1 Timothy 6:7-8, 10-12).

Trust Me, My child. Claim the peace that only I can offer. My Son does not give peace as the world gives peace. Use your worry over money to lift up prayers for your financial security, and I will answer. Live simply that others may simply live.

And do not envy the wealthy. "Truly I tell you, it is hard for someone who is rich to enter the kingdom of heaven. Again I tell you; it is easier for a camel to go through the eye of a needle than for someone who is rich to enter the kingdom of God" (Matthew 19:23). Where your heart is, you will find your God.

My Prayer

Father in heaven, thank you for your many blessings. "Keep falsehood and lies far from me; give me neither poverty nor riches, but give me only my daily bread. Otherwise, I may have too much and disown you and say, 'Who is the LORD?'" (Proverbs 30:8-9).

Father, continue to see that I have what I need, and if there be an abundance, I will give You thanks by seeking ways to do good works (2 Corinthians 9:8). All my blessings are signs of Your goodness and care. All gifts are only loaned that I may take the ten pieces of silver and make ten more by sharing it with others. Help me to see beyond the material things of this world to the One who made the world and everything within it. Help me to live simply.

I need confession here, Lord, because You know how concern for money and efforts to increase my material possessions have at times taken over my life. I have fixed my mind on something new: a car, purse, home, article of clothing, type of shoe, vacation, piece of jewelry, prestigious school, or an item for my special hobby or sport. Having fixed my mind on something, I've often allowed possession to consume my mind. Not any of the things I wanted were bad. Sometimes they were things I or my family could legitimately use. But in all honesty, Lord, I know that getting something I did

*not own did tend to displace my focus from You. The more
I am consumed with possessions, the less room in my heart
for You, the living God.*

*Money and material possessions have been cause for envy
and jealousy. I've coveted the possessions of others, especially their homes or cars or financial security. I've found
myself resenting or envying what others have. Why should
they have more? They don't work harder than I do. They
may even have little or no faith in God, so why should You
bless them so?*

*I begin to grow suspicious of the means others used to
achieve what they have. I search for evidence of some
misdeed or greed on their part that served their material
well-being. I become covetous. It is not just what others
own that breeds this jealousy. Why are they thinner than
I am? Or better looking? Or healthier, more athletic? Why
can they play an instrument or sing, and I was denied these
gifts? Why are their children so talented and successful and
mine ordinary?*

*"But if you harbor bitter envy and selfish ambition in your
hearts, do not boast about it or deny the truth. Such 'wisdom' does not come down from heaven but is earthly, un-
spiritual, demonic" (James 3:14-15).*

*I have wished bad things on those I've been covetous or
jealous of. I've thought that it would give me pleasure if
they were stripped of their gifts and made equal to me.
This is sin. It is evil. I sincerely repent. I commit myself to
celebrate the gifts and blessings of others. Help me not to
judge or compare. Help me, Lord, to be genuinely happy
and satisfied with the unique persons You designed me and
my children to be. Let gratitude born of the Spirit push out
jealousy from my soul and fill me with light and peace.*

Father, help me to recognize that I not only have enough, but I have been richly blessed. Give me a grateful heart and let me never tire in giving You thanks. Through Christ our Lord, I pray.

Spoken in the Spirit through Jesus, the Son, to the Father. Amen.

CHAPTER 21

THE POWER OF FORGIVENESS

God is speaking to you. Listen!

Forgiveness is at the heart of My teaching. Forgiveness is not just a suggestion or an option; it is a commandment. "For if you forgive other people when they sin against you, your heavenly Father will also forgive you. But if you do not forgive others their sins, your Father will not forgive your sins" (Matthew 6:14-15).

You may find it hard to forgive those who have hurt you deeply, but remember, I forgave you. Every time you seek My forgiveness, I grant it without hesitation. I do not keep a record of your wrongs. "As far as the east is from the west, so far has he removed our transgressions from us" (Psalm 103:12). My mercy is infinite, and I call you to reflect that mercy in your own life.

When you refuse to forgive, you imprison yourself. The bitterness and resentment that grow within you can poison your spirit, creating a barrier between you and the peace I desire for you. "Get rid of all bitterness, rage, and anger, brawling and slander, along with every form of malice, Be kind and compassionate to one another, forgiving each other, just as in Christ God forgave you" (Ephesians 4:31-32). "Bear with each other and forgive one another if any of you has a grievance against someone. Forgive as the Lord forgave you" (Colossians 3:13)

Forgiveness does not mean excusing wrong behavior or pretending that nothing happened. It is an act of letting go of the right to hold onto anger and the desire for revenge. It is releasing the burden of judgment to Me, trusting that I will deal with the situation in My own way and time. "Do not take revenge, my dear friends, but leave room for God's wrath, for it is written: 'It is mine to avenge; I will repay,' says the Lord" (Romans 12:19).

Forgiving others is a process that may take time. It often requires you to revisit the hurt and release it over and over again. But as you continue to forgive, you will find that the grip of the past loosens, and you will experience the freedom that only My Spirit can bring. Remember, I am with you in this journey. I will give you the strength and grace you need to forgive, even when it feels impossible. "I can do all things through him who gives me strength" (Philippians 4:13).

Forgiveness is also about healing. It heals your heart and mind, and it opens the door for relationships to be restored. Even if the other person never asks for your forgiveness or acknowledges their wrong, your decision to forgive will bring healing and peace to your own soul. "Above all, love each other deeply, because love covers over a multitude of sins" (1 Peter 4:8).

Embrace the power of forgiveness. It is the key to unlocking the fullness of life that I have promised you. Trust in My justice, rest in My peace, and let go of the hurt that has weighed you down. Your freedom and healing are My gifts to you when you choose to forgive.

My Prayer

Father, I come to You with a heart that has been wounded by others. I confess that I have held onto resentment, anger, and bitterness. I know that these feelings have separated me from Your peace and love, and I desire to be free from them. Please help me to forgive as You have forgiven me. "The righteous cry out, and the LORD hears them; he delivers them from all their troubles. The LORD is close to the brokenhearted and saves those who are crushed in spirit" (Psalm 34:17-18)

I acknowledge that forgiveness is not easy, Lord. The hurt I have experienced feels so deep, and I am afraid to let go of it. But I also know that holding onto this pain is not what You want for me. You desire that I live in the freedom that comes from forgiving others. So, I ask You, Lord, to give me the strength and grace to forgive.

Your word says that You are just, and that vengeance belongs to You, not to me. Help me to trust in Your justice and to release my desire for revenge. I surrender my pain, my hurt, and my anger to You, and I ask You to heal my heart.

Father, I also pray for those who have hurt me. I ask that You bless them and lead them to repentance. I release them from my judgment and place them in Your hands. May Your will be done in their lives.

Thank You, Lord, for the gift of forgiveness. Thank You for forgiving me every time I come to You in repentance. I am grateful that Your mercy is new every morning, and that I can walk in the freedom of Your grace.

Help me, Father, to continue forgiving, even when it is hard. Let Your love flow through me, covering over every sin and hurt. Fill me with Your peace and joy, so that I may reflect Your love to others.

Spoken in the Spirit through Jesus, the Son, to the Father. Amen.

CHAPTER 22

HEALING THE BROKENHEARTED

God is speaking to you. Listen!

I see your pain, and I know your sorrow. The wounds you carry may be hidden from others, but they are not hidden from Me. I am the God who heals, and I am here to bind up your broken heart. "He heals the brokenhearted and binds up their wounds" (Psalm 147:3).

The world is full of suffering, and at times, it may seem overwhelming. But know this: I am close to the brokenhearted. "The Lord is close to the brokenhearted and saves those who are crushed in spirit" (Psalm 34:18). Your pain does not go unnoticed, and your tears are not forgotten. "Record my misery; lists my tears on your scroll—are they not in your record?" (Psalm 56:8).

I invite you to bring your pain to Me. Do not hold back your tears or your cries. Pour out your heart before Me, and I will comfort you. "Cast all your anxiety on him because he cares for you" (1 Peter 5:7). I understand your suffering, and I am with you in the midst of it.

Healing takes time, but I promise to be with you every step of the way. Trust in My timing and My process. I am working all things together for your good, even when it is difficult to see. "And we know that in all things God works for the good of those who love him, who have been called according to his purpose" (Romans 8:28). "He will wipe every tear from their eyes. There will be no more death or mourning or crying or pain, for the old order of things has passed away" (Revelation 21:4)

Your broken heart will not remain broken forever. I will bring beauty from your pain, joy from your mourning, and praise from your despair. God has anointed the psalmist "to comfort all who mourn, and provide for those who grieve in Zion—to bestow on them a crown of beauty instead of ashes, the oil of joy instead of mourning, and a garment of praise instead of a spirit of despair" (Isaiah 61:2-3).

Lean on Me, and let Me carry you through this season of brokenness. You do not have to bear this burden alone. I am your refuge and strength, an ever-present help in trouble. "God is our refuge and strength, an ever-present help in trouble" (Psalm 46:1).

As you walk with Me through the valley of the shadow of death, fear no evil, for I am with you. My rod and My staff will comfort you. "Even though I walk through the darkest valley, I will fear no evil, for you are with me; your rod and your staff, they comfort me" (Psalm 23:4).

Hold onto My promises, for they are true and faithful. I will heal your heart, restore your soul, and bring you into a place of peace and wholeness. "Peace I leave with you; my peace I give you. I do not give to you as the world gives. Do not let your hearts be troubled and do not be afraid" (John 14:27).

My Prayer

Father, I come to You with a heart that is heavy and broken. The pain I feel is deep, and I am struggling to carry it on my own. I need Your healing touch. I need Your comfort and peace.

Lord, I know that You see my pain, and I am grateful that I do not have to hide it from You. I pour out my heart before You, trusting that You care for me and that You are near to the brokenhearted. Please bind up my wounds, and heal my broken heart.

Help me to trust in Your timing, Lord. I know that healing is a process, and I ask for the patience and faith to walk through it with You. Give me the strength to endure this season of pain, and help me to see the beauty that You will bring from it.

I place my trust in Your promises, Father. I believe that You are working all things together for my good, even when I cannot see it. I choose to believe that You will turn my mourning into joy, my ashes into beauty, and my despair into praise.

Thank You, Lord, for being my refuge and strength. Thank You for walking with me through this valley and for comforting me with Your presence. I am grateful that I do not have to bear this burden alone, and that You are always with me.

Please give me Your peace, Lord. The peace that surpasses all understanding, the peace that the world cannot give. Let it guard my heart and mind as I continue to trust in You.

Spoken in the Spirit through Jesus, the Son, to the Father. Amen.

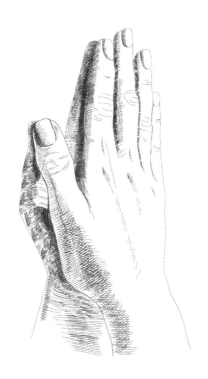

CHAPTER 23

HEALING

God is speaking. Listen!

My children, I hear your prayers for healing. You wonder when I will answer. Did it ever occur to you that all your prayers of petition, aside from prayers of worship and thanksgiving, deal with something broken? A broken mind or body, heart or relationship, a broken promise. Many times, it is your relationship with Me that is broken, and you seek to restore it.

Often it is your relationships with other people that are broken, and you seek reconciliation. Couples pray for help with communication, resolving major decisions, falling out of love, finances, values, and infidelity. Parents pray for help with broken children. Children can act out their unresolved struggles, refuse to live with rules, keep bad company, act out in tantrums, develop addictions, and some absolutely refuse to comply with the simplest requests, making daily living a nightmare.

Prayers rise before Me from people with broken relationships. Parents age, and adult children experience stress and anger, exhausted with their care. Friends have issues with one another. There are an infinite number of factors as personalities generate misunderstanding and conflict. War, racism, and slavery are more ugly manifestations of broken relationships. Your relationships with others contribute a great deal to your sense of well-being and happiness. And just as you pray for healing with broken relationships with others, sometimes the brokenness is within your own heart. You may be broken in many ways.

I wonder if you ever considered that your relationship with the environment is broken too. As a human family, you are polluting the earth and seas, burning the forests, and killing off other living species. You were placed in the garden to be its stewards, not to burn it down and kill the animals and birds. All kinds of physical, mental, and even spiritual maladies afflict you. Everything seems to be broken! It is for all these different types of brokenness that you seek healing.

I am blamed a great deal for not answering your prayers. You keep the commandments, try as best you can to love Me, and try to love your neighbor, work hard to follow the teachings of Jesus, and so you wonder why your prayers concerning the most important parts of your life seem to go unanswered.

Many interpret My delay as a sign of My indifference to your suffering. They conclude I am unfair or uncaring. I would like to invite you to consider another perspective on My apparent indifference. Imagine a sixteen-year-old boy deliberately dropping a dish. It smashes. He looks up at his mother. He doesn't say "I'm sorry." He says, "Fix it!"

I know you are probably wondering what My little story about a dish has to do with Me not answering your prayers, so let Me try to explain with yet another story, the story of the garden and your first parents who deliberately broke the dish.

The characters in the story are Adam and Eve, the serpent, and Me. This particular story is pregnant with meaning. Ponder it in your heart. Adam and Eve had a unique relationship with "Us." They knew nothing of Father, Son, and Spirit. They knew Us as One. They "walked" with Us through the garden, spoke with Us as a friend, trusted Us and loved Us. We and they, together knew only peace and harmony.

I made one condition on their life with Me in Eden. There were countless numbers of trees in the Garden. I forbade them to eat from the fruit of one tree, the one that grew in the middle. You would think that given the vast expanse of Eden; your parents would never think of this one tree again. That's not what happened.

They began to think about this one tree all the time. They asked themselves more and more questions about this tree and about Me. What was My motivation for making this rule? Was I telling them the truth? Essentially, the questions asked if I could be trusted. Was I holding something back that could increase their knowledge and power? Did I not want them to better themselves and grow?

You might ask why they might need more knowledge or power or food, for that matter. I had provided for all their needs and gave them no cause to question My word. Their questions reached out into the deepest depths of the forest and summoned the serpent. Their doubt in My word had diminished the value and esteem in which they held our relationship. They gave their full attention to the serpent. They listened to the serpent's voice. They accepted the serpent's truth and acted on the serpent's advice.

Four things changed after they ate the fruit from the forbidden tree, and all of them had to do with relationships. Their relationship with Me changed first. They rejected My voice as trustworthy, and then they hid when they heard Me in the garden. They were My friends, and they trusted Me. Now, they hide.

Second, their relationship with one another was broken. Adam blamed Eve. Eve blamed the serpent. Third, their relationship with their own selves was broken. Now they felt shame, disappointment, guilt, anger, and rejection. Fourth, their relationship with My creation was broken. Food was no longer given freely by Mother Nature. Adam and Eve had to till the earth. The animals now bite and sting. They suffer from the weather and need clothing. They get sick and die.

"Sin" is the word you use to cover all the dimensions involved in the brokenness that followed. The original communion we shared, our oneness, our unity fractured. The sin that entered the world not only broke our friendship, but it gave birth to mortality and crushed the original harmony that characterized the life we knew together in Eden.

Look into the deepest recesses of your mind for the memory of this story. You are born not just with an individual consciousness but also with a corporate consciousness. The Holy Spirit is with you now. The Spirit came precisely to lead you to all truth. The Spirit will validate the essential truths of this story. You, human, were made to be in communion with other humans and with Me. This is who you are, a being who exists in relationship. You were never intended to exist on your own. You were created to be one with Me, with others, with yourself, and with all creation.

The message of the story concerns the breaking of our original communion. You, made in My image and likeness, are defined by your connections to Me, others, and yourself. You are made for communion. Now ask yourself who is responsible for the brokenness in the world. Turn within to the Spirit.

Adam and Eve were not alone responsible. All are party to the brokenness. It is because of this shared responsibility that you must all share in the restoration, share in the work of picking up the broken pieces.

So back to the original question: Why am I not answering your prayers for healing? The simple response is that you and your brothers and sisters must all have a part in the restoration. I will not act on My own. "Truly I tell you, if you had faith as small as a mustard seed, you can say to this mountain, 'Move from here to there,' and it will move. Nothing will be impossible for you" (Matthew 17:20). In other words, your faith works when functioning in communion with Me. I choose you to be party to healing, to making things right again. The first step in that whole process is to choose My voice over others.

> *"Therefore, just as sin entered the world through one man, and death through sin, in this way death came to all people, because all sinned."*
>
> Romans 5:12

I have taken the single most important step toward the restoration of our original communion. I, the Word you had rejected, came to earth. I lived side by side with you. I spoke with you again as we did in the Garden, and we walked together. I offered you My friendship. I died on your behalf on the cross for the forgiveness of your sins.

The path to healing, the restoration, and the coming of the kingdom has six stages:

1. **Own your responsibility!** Admit that "sin" belongs to you as a human. You opened your heart to another voice besides the Word made flesh, My Son! Be honest. Has My voice always been enough? Have you trusted Me, walked with Me, been a friend to Me? Have you questioned Our plan, Our goodness? Have your questions diminished your ability to trust My voice and summoned the prince of this world?

2. **Admit the truth.** You pushed Us away from your side and gave that place to another, and it was Our absence, Our silence that allowed the other voice to speak and be heard. You must bring Us back into your heart. It is Our presence, Our strength, Our being you need. You were not fashioned to make the life journey on your own. We were to be partners from the beginning. You were to be one with other humans from your creation and one with Me.

   Only when Moses' hands were raised in prayer to the God of Abraham did the battle against Amalek go in favor of Israel. As soon as Moses tired and lowered his hands, as soon as he stopped reaching out to God, the battle turned, and evil grew in power. "Seek the Lord while he may be found; call on him while he is near" (Isaiah 55:6). "My flesh and my heart may fail, but God is the strength of my heart and my portion forever" (Psalm 73:26).

3. **Acknowledge that It Is Our Will to Heal.** It is Who "I Am." "Worship the LORD your God, and his blessing will be on your food and water. I will take away sickness from among you, and none will miscarry or be barren in your land. I will give you a full life span" (Exodus 23:25-26). "'For I know the plans I have for you,' declares the LORD, 'plans to prosper you and not to harm you, plans to give you hope and a future. Then you will call on me and

come and pray to me, and I will listen to you. You will seek me and find me when you seek me with all your heart'" (Jeremiah 29:11-14).

4. **Summon Us with the Name I revealed to you, the all-powerful, Jesus.** With faith and trust, proclaim Jesus to be your Savior. "That at the name of Jesus every knee should bow, in heaven and on earth and under the earth, and every tongue acknowledge that Jesus Christ is Lord, to the glory of God the Father" (Philippians 2:10-11). Bring Jesus back into your story. Renounce all voices but the voice of the Word made flesh.

5. **Surrender yourself to the Word of Jesus.** Place Him on the throne of your heart. Love Him, keep His commandments, and love your brother and sister as yourself.

Take to yourself the cross, and that will mark your surrender to My Son. "Then Jesus said to his disciples, 'Whoever wants to be my disciple must deny themselves and take up their cross and follow me. For whoever wants to save their life will lose it, but whoever loses their life for me will find it'" (Matthew 16:24-25). "Come to me, all you who are weary and burdened, and I will give you rest. Take my yoke upon you and learn from me, for I am gentle and humble in heart, and you will find rest for your souls. For my yoke is easy and my burden is light" (Matthew 11:28-30).

6. **Pray.** Your restoration into communion with Jesus in the Spirit will ripple out on ocean currents through the universe. Note how often Jesus prayed and that act brought forth healing. Paul is also an example of the role of prayer in healing. Recall how often he prayed. We came as Spirit cast darkness away and brought healing. "Do not be anxious about anything, but in every situation,

by prayer and petition, with thanksgiving, present your requests to God. And the peace of God, which transcends all understanding, will guard your hearts and your minds in Christ Jesus" (Philippians 4:6-7).

Pray alone and pray with your church community. Together. "Is anyone among you in trouble? Let them pray. Is anyone happy? Let them sing songs of praise. Is anyone among you sick? Let them call the elders of the church to pray over them and anoint them with oil in the name of the Lord. And the prayer offered in faith will make the sick person well; the Lord will raise them up. If they have sinned, they will be forgiven" (James 5:13-15).

My Prayer

Lord God, Father, Son, and Spirit, please hear the groanings of my heart. There have been times I have questioned not just Your words in Scripture but Your very existence. Is there a God, or am I alone? Is this all there is? Can anyone hear me? Is God real, or am I just fooling myself because of my fear? Am I really and truly alone? I see this prayer for healing, Lord, as a way of voiding these questions and reminding me that You are with me always. I need to reaffirm that Your divine presence, the friendship of Jesus and the Holy Spirit, lives within me through my faith and baptism.

I am torn apart by the suffering I see. Pain wracks the body and mind. Pills fail to cover the agony, and life seems to drain away. Just picking up my head or walking to the bathroom takes every bit of my strength. Fear of what tomorrow brings adds weight to the torment. Losing not only one's physical strength but my mind terrifies me. Dementia,

Parkinson's, Alzheimer's, ALS, muscular dystrophy, cystic fibrosis, and on and on goes the range of things that go wrong. Add to this the brokenness, defeat, or rage in cities around the world. You alone know the body and mind, Lord God, but more—You made us. It is You alone who knows how to restore us. I stand on the promise of Your Word and ask, plea, and beg for mercy and healing.

Childhood and genetic diseases break our hearts as we see the youngest and most helpless slowly weaken and fail to thrive. Dreams are shattered. Hearts are broken. Tears flow as parents stand before the wasting bodies of their children.

Physical and mental anguish leads some to give up and despair. Some feel they can't go on. Suicide today is like a plague that proliferates everywhere, especially afflicting our youth and the elderly. Grief is the new pandemic. We bury our dreams and hopes, our spouses and children. We bury our careers, our marriages, our youth, and our health.

Job's experience of having everyone and everything one loves stripped from his life is shared by more and more people. We sit with our bodies and minds covered in sores, anguish, and emptiness. We feel robbed and cheated. We think ourselves abandoned and ashamed. Are we forsaken?

From my flesh, I know I will see You, O Lord God. I know You will allow me to stand again upon the dust and sing Your praise. You will raise me up together with all those I have loved. You will call us forth from the pit, and we shall laugh again.

Today, Father, I surrender myself and those for whom I pray to Your holy will. If it is Your will—and I hope it is— then I am asking You, Lord, to restore the physical and mental health of those I name this hour. Resolve their many problems, lift their torment, bring them the peace that You alone can give. Shine the light of hope upon them once again.

I pray for the human family. If nations would use their wealth for medical research instead of arms, all disease would already have been resolved. It is our brokenness that continues to feed disease, not Your apathy, Almighty Lord.

Restore the damaged relationship I and others have with You, Lord God. Restore the communion of the human family. End division, hate, war, starvation, and homelessness. Help us reach out as a family to the migrant and the displaced by war. Help integrate foreign-born people into the community and protect citizens from those pathological migrants who terrorize, murder, and rape the innocent.

Restore our bodies, minds, and spirits. Come, Word of God, and create anew what we have broken or destroyed. Let every person discover the peace that You alone can give, Lord Jesus.

If there are financial concerns or relationship issues that weigh on people's hearts, I pray that You lift these burdens. Take away the horrific plague of depression, anxiety, and all forms of physical, mental, or spiritual affliction. Send upon us the light of Your Holy Spirit. Let Your light cast all darkness away and restore all we have broken. Let us be friends again, Lord, with both You and one another. May I, as an individual, and people everywhere surrender to You as Lord God, the One who made us and called us forth.

Most of all, Lord, I ask for the gift of faith. Faith not only for myself (I believe; help my unbelief), but I pray for the gift of faith for those I love and for people everywhere. May all come to know You, Jesus, and love You. May we all see You as You are, the living Word of God, preexistent Creator, Savior, and Redeemer.

All glory to You, Lord God of hosts, King of all creation.

Spoken in the Spirit through Jesus, the Son, to the Father. Amen.

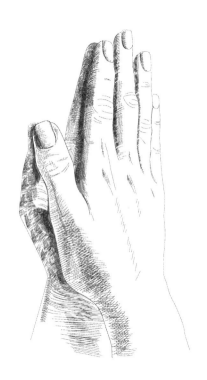

CHAPTER 24

THE HARDEST LEAP IS INTO GOD'S ARMS

God is speaking to you. Listen!

My dear child, I am glad you are here! The hardest leap into the unknown is the leap into My arms. Faith is like jumping off a cliff and not knowing if someone is at the bottom with open arms to catch you. To trust is to believe that I will do what is expected. Expect Me to catch you and love you.

Adam and Eve walked with Me in the garden of Eden. You know the story. I told them not to eat the fruit in the middle of the garden. They couldn't stop thinking about that tree. Was I telling them the truth? Did I have other motives? They no longer trusted in Me. They shut out My voice, My words. They did, however, trust the serpent. They chose his voice over Mine. They began in My arms and leaped away.

Abraham is called the "Father of Faith." He was told he would be the father of a host of nations. "Abraham fell face-down; he laughed and said to himself, 'Will a son be born to a man a hundred years old? Will Sarah bear a child at the age of ninety?'" (Genesis 17:17). Yes, to every rational mind,

My promise was crazy, yet Abraham made that leap into My arms. He believed Me. Sarah would have a child.

I sent My angel, Gabriel, to Mary. The angel told Mary she would conceive a child, My child, a child with no human father. Impossible! How would a baby come without a father? Would Mary be stoned with no husband? What would her parents think? "No" would have been a reasonable response, but she chose to leap into My arms and trusted. "'I am the Lord's servant,' Mary answered. 'May your word to me be fulfilled'" (Luke 1:38). The unknown terrified Mary, but she leaped anyway.

Naaman was a pagan commander in the service of the king of Aram. Naaman had leprosy. His slave girl told him of a great prophet in Israel who cured leprosy. Naaman solicited a letter of introduction from the king of Aram, prepared a great treasure as a gift, and traveled to see this prophet he heard cures leprosy. The prophet's name was Elisha. The king of Israel met with Naaman first and was convinced this ridiculous request for a miracle was only a plot to start a war.

Elisha heard what was going on and sent word to have Naaman come to his home. Naaman repeated his request to Elisha and received his instructions from the prophet. "Wash seven times in the Jordan River." Naaman couldn't believe how ridiculous these instructions sounded! There were huge rivers in his own country with clean water, much better than any river in Israel. If washing in a river is all that is necessary, he could have just stayed home! And besides, if this God of Israel is a god at all, why wash seven times? Why not just once? Why not just skip the wash and command the body to heal? You can imagine what went through Naaman's mind. He was angry and turned to go home. His servants intervened and tried to convince him that he had nothing to lose. Naaman relented. He washed seven times in the

Jordan. Naaman trusted the word of Elisha, that is the word of Israel's God. In one act, Naaman renounced his gods and leaped into My arms. He was healed.

Naaman sounds a great deal like many people today who don't feel any need to join a community to worship Me on the Sabbath. Why do I need to worship God with others when I can pray alone in my backyard, looking at the trees and birds? These individuals don't seem to hear Me calling people together, into communion with one another and with Me. They don't really believe My Word. They don't really trust Me.

No one was closer to Me than My Son, Jesus, and even He was tested. The night before His crucifixion, Jesus went to Gethsemane. He was in agony over what was about to transpire. He prayed, "My soul is sorrowful even to death. . . . He fell prostrate in prayer, saying 'My Father, if it is possible, may this cup be taken from me. Yet not as I will, but as you will'" (Matthew 26:39). So deep was His agony that Jesus' sweat was like drops of blood. Death is always a leap into the unknown. Terrifying. Jesus trusted and leapt into my arms from the cross.

The only prayer My Son taught you mirrors His own actions in the garden. "Thy will be done." Yes, you take the leap into life and ultimately into death, not completely sure of what will come, but you choose to believe that I will be there to catch you. Even if it is your dead body I catch and lay in a grave. "Trust in the LORD with all your heart and lean not on your own understanding; in all your ways submit to him, and he will make your paths straight" (Proverbs 3:5-6). Jesus told Martha, "I am the resurrection and the life. The one who believes in me will live, even though they die; and whoever lives by believing in me will never die" (John 11:25). Do you believe this?

My Prayer

Jesus, Word of God, I think You know how hard it is to trust.

I have some pretty extensive experience with trust, Lord. I've trusted friends, close friends, people who I knew loved me, people I loved, and then, over what amounts to a triviality, they threw me away. I didn't count. I guess our friendship only existed in my mind. I believed we were friends. I trusted them with my secrets. They threw me away! You know how much that hurt? I don't think I'm over it yet. Please, Lord, don't throw me away!

I trusted You, Lord, that I would find fellowship and communion within a church community. I just found little, stupid, petty people. I trusted our justice system to do what was right, and I see over and over again that one gets as much justice as they can afford. I look at the Jews who trusted in Your covenant, believed in Your love, and six million died in the Holocaust. I mean, Jesus, with so much evidence that trust often fails, why should I fool myself and believe that You are with me?

I stop here. Take a breath. Reflect on my life. I search my experience and collect my thoughts.

I guess all my frustration is based on the short version of the story, the short version being life on earth. This life is only a test. This is not my home, Lord. The full story needs to stretch out and include eternity, Your kingdom. "But our citizenship is in heaven. And we eagerly await a Savior from there, the Lord Jesus Christ, who, by the power that enables him to bring everything under his control, will transform our lowly bodies so that they will be like his glorious body" (Philippians 3:20-21).

Blessed be You, my God and Father. In Your great mercy, You gave me a new birth to a living hope in Jesus. I choose to believe Your story is true. I do have an inheritance that is imperishable, undefiled, and unfading, kept in heaven. I know that as I make my journey toward communion with the Father, I will be tested. I will suffer various trials, but as gold is tested in fire, You are refining me, burning away impurities that I may prove worthy to praise, glory, and honor the Lamb that was slain. I have not seen Him, yet I love Him. I believe in Him.

Yes, I have stories of suffering, but if truth be told, I have also witnessed Your miracles. A baby is born. An incurable disease goes into remission. Marriages that were poison became wells of living water. Churches torn apart with bickering come together to minister to the hungry or send missionaries into the world. Forgiveness is offered after betrayal. Broken friendships are restored. And, yes, Lord, the dead do live on because Your word is true. You are the resurrection and the life.

Lord, I know someone inside the gates of Your kingdom who is waiting for me right now. Thank You for allowing me to experience the presence of someone I love who has passed from this life. I am grateful for the peace and comfort Your Spirit brings.

Jesus, I heard You speak: "Look, I am coming soon! My reward is with me, and I will give to each person according to what they have done. I am the Alpha and the Omega, the First and the Last, the Beginning and the End" (Revelation 22:12-13).

I have always been afraid of heights, Lord, so You know any leap into the unknown is difficult. I stand in the trust and power of Your Word that has come to me. The voice of Jesus is real, and it is true. Jesus is risen. I jump. The hardest, the longest leap of my life is the one I take into Your arms, Lord. Thank You for catching me. I know You are here.

Glory be to the Father and to the Son and to the Holy Spirit.

Spoken in the Spirit through Jesus, the Son, to the Father. Amen.

CHAPTER 25

THE TRINITY: FATHER, SON, AND HOLY SPIRIT

God is speaking. Listen!

Jesus taught you that you would know His disciples by their love for Me and for one another. How could it come to pass that people who called themselves Christians murdered one another, arguing about words to describe My triune existence? Did they not know that all their talk was gobbledygook, meaningless babble? Even with My coming to earth in human form as Jesus, you still do not know Me. You cannot fathom the depth of My nature or My Being with words. St. Augustine said it best, "God is not what you imagine or what you think you understand. If you understand, you have failed." "If you understand, it is not God."

I am beyond your capacity to imagine or describe. I am God. I am love. I am good. I am unchanging and immeasurable. I am hope. I am Creator. I am unfathomable.

"'For my thoughts are not your thoughts, neither are your ways my ways,' declares the LORD. 'As

*the heavens are higher than the earth, so are my
ways higher than your ways and my thoughts
than your thoughts.'"*

Isaiah 55:8-9

The identity of a woman as wife, mother, and friend may
offer you a glimpse of who I am and why I am unknowable.
Imagine a married woman with three small children working
outside the home. Her husband knows this woman as wife.
She is his spouse, friend, confidant, lover, and partner. His
relationship with this woman is unique. Her children know
her as Mommy. This is the person they first think of when
they want a cookie, cut their knee, or have an argument with
a schoolmate. The woman's coworkers know this same person as a friend. They see her as disciplined, hardworking,
shy, easy to get along with, cooperative, and helpful. The
woman has three titles: Wife, Mommy, and Friend. She is
known in three completely different ways by three groups of
people. One might even say she is known as three different
persons. Yet the woman is only one person.

You know Me, your Creator, in three different ways: as
Father; as Son in Jesus; and as Holy Spirit. We are One, a
pure relationship. You are made in Our image and likeness.
So as the creatures made in Our image, your innermost nature, your being, is defined by My definition. Your existence
and your identity as a human being are defined by your relationships. You exist in relationship with Me, your God. You
exist in your relationships with other humans. Part of your
identity as a unique person is the relationship you have with
yourself—your body, mind, and spirit. Last of all, you exist in
relationship to the created universe. You exist as an infinite
number of connections through your relationships.

Your relationships are constantly changing. You are changing. Sometimes the word "becoming" is used to describe this evolution, this journey. You are following a plan I devised in ages past. Your destiny is to be transformed into one who might stand before Me in My kingdom and share in My glory. Even now, you are being born anew. You are being readied for your marriage to the Bridegroom. You have been chosen and called, predestined and justified to become one with Us. Communion with Us is your destiny.

You only know Us through what We do, as a hazy reflection in a mirror. Even with Our coming to earth in Jesus, you still do not fully know Him or Us. You know Jesus's human face and even hear His divine words. You love Him and open yourself to His Spirit. He dwells within you, and you in Him. But still, Jesus, the Christ, stands outside of time, and you are bound to it. He exists outside the universe, and you are its prisoner.

Christ preexisted the known universe and brought it into being. You see Us as a burning bush, an angel, a man, a cloud, natural cataclysms, a gentle breeze, and a pillar of fire. In Jesus, you see Our human face and a resurrected body. You know Him, but still, you do not know Him or Us. We have revealed Ourselves in three different ways to cater to the smallness of your nature. Do not be proud or haughty. Though We are these three faces—Father, Son, and Spirit—We are not these three faces. We are more. Though We are three Persons, We are not three persons. We cannot be confined to words bound by the finiteness of your languages. We are One God. There is no other.

My Prayer

Father, Son, and Holy Spirit, I stand in awe and wonder before Your mighty presence. Who am I to dare speak to One who is so mighty? I bless You for allowing my lips to speak Your praise and tell of Your mighty deeds.

Almighty God, You are love (1 John 4:16). You are the good shepherd (John 10), the bread of life (John 6), the Creator (John 1), the alpha and the omega, the beginning and the end (Revelation 22:13). You are hope (Romans 15:13). You are holy (Leviticus 11:44). I know You, Holy God, and I do not know You. You are indescribable and incomprehensible.

My mind is limited to my experience and my imagination, and both are bound by my brain and my spirit. You chose to unveil Your presence over the centuries to an ever-changing humankind. Together we humans have been growing, evolving. I, as an individual, knew You differently at twenty than I did at ten, and I will know You differently yet again as I age and grow in wisdom.

The Scriptures trace the history of Your revelation to Israel and to the followers of Jesus as Father, Son, and Holy Spirit. Our understanding of You has evolved as Your revelation proceeded. Today, following the writing of Scripture, Your Holy Spirit continues to speak Your truth.

Jesus promised the Spirit would guide us to all truth. Jesus tells us: "I have much more to say to you, more than you can now bear. But when he, the spirit of truth, comes, he will guide you into all the truth. He will not speak on his own; he will speak only what he hears, and he will tell you what is yet to come. He will glorify me because it is from me that he will receive what he will make known to you.

All that belongs to the Father is mine. That is why I said the Spirit will receive from me what he will make known to you" (John 16:12-15). Thank You, Elohim, for the gift of Your Spirit. Thank You for refusing to be silent. Thank you for guiding Your church in the ages that followed the resurrection with the voice of Your Spirit. You speak in every age to Your people. "The LORD himself goes before you and will be with you; he will never leave you nor forsake you. Do not be afraid; do not be discouraged" (Deuteronomy 31:8).

Father, I give my life over to Your Spirit that I may be more like Christ. Thank You for the gift of faith in Your Son. I bow before You in worship and sing Your praise. You are God, and there is no other.

Thank You, El Shaddai, for showing me Your three Persons as Father, Son, and Spirit. I understand that these words do not hold Your essence or being. You are three Persons, and You are not three Persons. You are One.

Glory be to the Father and to the Son and to the Holy Spirit now and forever.

Spoken in the Spirit through Jesus, the Son, to the Father. Amen.

CHAPTER 26

HOPE IN GOD

God is speaking to you. Listen!

I love the word hope. It is the optimistic expectation that things will work out. Everything is going to be alright. You hope when you "cherish a desire with anticipation."

You accepted My Son, Jesus, as your Savior, so you know you have been chosen. My Spirit spoke to your heart. It is true that you are on a journey that was planned for you from before your birth. You took My hand and began walking by My side, just like your first parents did in Eden. You allow Me to lead.

This journey is much more than a journey to a place, My kingdom, but rather it is a journey to Me, to God. You were made to know Me and love Me. Your glorification awaits you. Yet, at the same time, your journey is to become the best version of yourself, the person I first imagined when I gave you a name.

I am your rock and refuge, your secure stronghold and fortress. I am your hope. From your mother's womb, I have been your guide (Psalm 71:3-6). A guide always has a destination.

You are being prepared to stand before My throne. "So you also must be ready because the Son of Man will come at an hour when you do not expect him" (Matthew 24:44).

I came to earth in Jesus just so you could see My face. You listened to My voice, and My Spirit was born inside you. I swept you up into My arms. I called you by name. I kissed you, breathed upon you, and My Spirit sang with joy within your soul.

My Holy Spirit speaks into the deepest recesses of your being. You know now that your life is larger than you ever imagined. Your life has a purpose. You were not born like the animals to eat, sleep, reproduce, and die. You were born to know Me, to become one with Me as Jesus is one with Me.

With the Spirit dwelling within you, there is an abiding expectation of something you cannot see, but yet you know is true. This is the birth of hope. With the Spirit, you know that My plan cannot be destroyed or corrupted. You yield to the Spirit and are swept up in a positive conviction that every incident going forward, both good and bad, every experience will work together for good.

"We know that in all things God works for the good of those who love him, who have been called according to his purpose" (Romans 8:28). You were chosen, predestined, called, justified, and soon, you will be glorified (Romans 8:28-30). The wondrous object of hope is your glorification! Your glorification marks your complete communion with Me. We will be one. Me in you and you in Us, Father, Son, and Spirit.

Life on earth is without meaning or purpose without Me. Human beings on their own cannot reach their own glorification. "With man this is impossible, but with God all things are possible" (Matthew 19:26).

My Prayer

My Savior Jesus, coming to know You is changing me. It was as if I had lived in a world of shadows, going through the motions, looking to my next meal, my next telephone conversation or chat, working, going out, cleaning up after myself, sleeping, and repeating these actions over and over again. I lived in a forest and never noticed the flowers. It never occurred to me that my life was empty, without purpose or meaning. I just didn't think about it. There was always laundry to do or some simple downtime to rest after becoming exhausted from a day at work. I realize now that everything I own or accumulate will one day pass away. Every person I care for will die. Time will just go on after my life ends, so my life would really be meaningless, but for You.

Something has happened to me with You, Jesus, in my life. It is as if Your Spirit took the sunglasses from my eyes. I see more clearly now. I see things as they are, not as I want them to be. Every day is filled with meaning and purpose. I discern Your design in every event and person. Everything is connected in some way.

There is another dimension to existence of which I was unaware before You came into my life, Jesus. I feel like my faith has brought me into the fold of an assembly of countless beings that spans not just time but all the cosmos. The journey of this present creation ends in You, Father. Thank You, Word of God. You spoke, and Your Spirit came forth to create and fill every atom and molecule, photon and quark, mind and body, spirit and soul with a piece of You. You are everywhere. Thank You for being in me!

Help me to prepare for Your coming, Lord God. With the Spirit, make me a child of the light and the day. Please continue to awaken me from this deep sleep of unknowing and disbelief. Let Your Word touch every part of my mind and heart that daily I might grow in faith and love (1 Thessalonians 5:2-6). Help me to be an authentic witness of Your love to others. Make my life honest, transparent, and genuinely good. "You are my refuge and my shield; I have put my hope in your word" (Psalm 119:114). Let that word continue to shape my thoughts, feelings, and actions.

As I continue in Your service, let me "always have hope; I will praise you more and more" (Psalm 71:14). You will come like a thief in the night, so come quickly, King Jesus, and take me to Yourself.

I rejoice in the truth of Your Word and the love You have shown me. The love You have shared with me does not delight in evil but rejoices with the truth. Let me feel in my own life Your love that protects, trusts, hopes, and perseveres (1 Corinthians 13:6-7).

Spirit of God, You are with me now. I feel You groaning, moaning this deep, painful longing for something wonderful. You want it to come quickly, as do I—that is, the glorification of humanity. My glorification. Everything is connected. Everything will be one again. Spirit, make me "joyful in hope, patient in affliction, and faithful in prayer" (Romans 12:12).

All glory to You, Word of God, Lord and Savior Jesus Christ.

Spoken in the Spirit through Jesus, the Son, to the Father. Amen.

CHAPTER 27

RELEASE YOUR BROTHER OR SISTER

God is speaking to you. Listen!

My children, you know Me as the all-powerful, mighty, holy ruler, and I am all of these. I use My power to do many things, but one role that truly brings Me great joy is the power to release you. I release you from the sin that binds you, from oppressors, from prison, from slavery, from addictions, from illness, from a heart of stone, from unforgiveness and revenge, from the grasp of evil, and from one way of living in the world that you might find the path I have set for you. You are made in My image and likeness. You, like Me, have power to release others. Consider imitating My power to release others who are bound.

I commanded Israel every seventh year to release debtors from their financial obligations. "At the end of every seven years you must cancel debts" (Deuteronomy 15:1). This was a way to lift a burden, to make living easier for those who were struggling. It gave people in debt some breathing room, a second chance. How have you acted to release others from these and similar burdens? You have power to lift burdens as citizens in democratic nations through your legislatures. As an individual, does anyone owe you money? If someone borrowed from you, it means they were having difficulties managing on their income before they approached you for the loan. Consider telling them that their debt is now a gift.

I commanded you to release those in need from their poverty (Deuteronomy 15:4). I have been gracious in My blessings to you, so use My example as a measure for your own gifts to others. I expressly said that sharing with others is one way you can give Me thanks for your blessings. Have you acted by releasing people from poverty? This was foremost in My Son's criteria to enter the kingdom at the last judgment.

You have emotional power over your children. Have you released your children from depending on you so that they can forge their own lives? Many of you need to be needed. There is a point, however, where providing for adult children cripples their ability to function as adults. By defending their dysfunction and by paying their bills, you are teaching your children to be helpless adults. Release your children from dependence. Insist they pay their own way. There is a time to stop picking up the pieces from your children's errors in judgment. Insist they solve their own problems. Stop offering them solutions. When they bring up their next crisis, simply tell them you believe they are gifted and intelligent and will eventually figure out how to solve their own problems. Release your children from depending on you! There is a time to say "No" and a time to let go.

Increasingly, you find yourselves in marriages that are toxic. Marital covenants involve not just financial assets but parental rights, visitation, and emotional freedom. How have you released your spouse from the marriage covenant and assisted them in a journey apart from yours? Yes, rejection is traumatic, devastating, a betrayal of your trust. Rejection is shattering, shaming, and murderous. There is never a time for revenge or spite. There is never a time when it is appropriate to try to destroy another's attempt to construct a new life. Release your spouse, however unfair or unjust it may be. Release them, though it hurts more than you care to admit. Release them on behalf of the emotional well-being of your children. Do not speak ill of your former spouse, especially to your children. Until you release your former spouse, it is you who remain chained.

It is supremely godlike when you can release a former spouse to another person so they might find love. Support your former spouse in their quest for happiness. Release yourself from resentment, bitterness, and a damaged sense of self-worth. Release yourself from seeking what is your due, justice. Be generous when they are selfish. Be kind when they seek your ruin. Release them from financial concerns or from having to abandon their children by demanding total custody. Set them free, and you will be unlocking chains that imprison both you and your children for years to come.

Do you release others and yourself from events of the past, the things of long ago that were painful and caused suffering? "Forget the former things; do not dwell on the past. See, I am doing a new thing! Now it springs up; do you not perceive it? I am making a way in the wilderness and streams in the wasteland" (Isaiah 43:18-19).

Children today do not remember record players when a vinyl disc rotated, and an arm with a needle fitted into small grooves as it turned. Often a scratch would occur on the vinyl, and the delicate needle would get stuck, repeating lines of music. By replaying events from the past over and over in your mind, you never move on to find the next note in your song. Your life is a melody, and each day has its own notes to play. Release yourself from events in the past. The past must not be given the power to define who you are today. Let it go. Use your power to release as did I and pray, "Give us this day our daily bread."

Release your tongue from deceitful speech, gossip, foul language, and detraction. "Keep your mouth free of perversity; keep corrupt talk far from your lips. Let your eyes look straight ahead; fix your gaze directly before you. Give careful thought to the paths for your feet and be steadfast in all your ways. Do not turn to the right or the left; keep your foot from evil" (Proverbs 4:24-27). You are powerful. You have the ability to make choices and to remake yourself. Remake yourself in the image of My Son, Jesus, and release habits of speech that feed the darkness. Be steadfast in your walk with Jesus.

I invite you to release those over whom you have power. Release has as many synonyms as you have experiences. By release, I mean escape from confinement, allow to leave, let out, deliver, rescue, emancipate, ransom, untie, unbridle, detach, unbind. When you release someone, they are free to act or move about freely. But more importantly, you are free when you release another.

But what if the person you release consistently returns to face you, and the relationship becomes even more toxic? The truth is, some people are not happy unless they are angry. There is no law in Scripture that insists you become a doormat for other people's abuse or use. I made you to love and be loved. I encourage you to be kind, and I demand that you refuse to be treated unkindly by others. You are My creation. You are precious. There is a time, however, to say, "No more" and avoid toxic people. Put them out of your life. This is not permission to inflict injury, but rather to protect you from mistreatment.

Hear Me, My child. Examine your life. I call upon you to release and unbind the chains that hold you and your neighbor bound.

My Prayer

Father, I hear You. You are asking me to enter the synagogue, go to the lectern, open the scroll of Isaiah, and put my feet into Jesus' sandals. You want me to witness the Lord's teaching and break the chains that bind others and myself. Give me the insight I need to see these chains and the courage and will to break them.

I know I cannot do this on my own. I have tried to do many of these things in the past and found them almost impossible. Holy Spirit, take over my mind, my body, and my spirit. Live in me. Move through my mouth and my hands. Form the words on my tongue that need to be said. Move my body to do what must be done. I need You, Spirit of Jesus, to take over. Help me to surrender my life to the teaching of Jesus.

Make me like Corrie Ten Boom. Her sister was mercilessly abused in a Nazi concentration camp, which led to her death. Corrie, herself a prisoner, was witness to these events. She knew the Nazi soldier responsible. The war ended. She wrote of her experience. She went out to lecture on her book.

One day, a stranger held out his open hand to congratulate Corrie on her book. He was the soldier responsible for her sister's death. At first, she was horror-struck and could not move, let alone shake the monster's hand. But You, Holy Spirit, took over. You released her from grief, trauma, from her rage at the violation of innocence. You, Holy Spirit, lifted Corrie's arm. You, Comforter, opened her hand. You, breath of God, touched her heart and shook the soldier's hand with Your own. Spirit of God, take over my life like that! Be one with me.

You call me to help people, and I do, but at the same time, some people are becoming unnecessarily dependent, and it is not good for them or for me. Come, Holy Spirit, and release me from the guilt that makes me feel I must help everyone all the time. Release me from my children, my relatives, and friends who make unjust demands when they need to take responsibility for their own lives. Even St. Paul had this problem when he advised, "The one who is unwilling to work shall not eat" (2 Thessalonians 3:10). Release me from the guilt that makes me feel unhealthy responsibility for fixing everyone's problems.

I know I must love everyone, but some people are tearing me down emotionally. Their presence is a dark pit that I feel sucking away my strength, my joy, my peace. Help me to release myself from the guilt that inhibits my ability to make decisions that protect me from darkness. Give me the courage and strength I need to move away from these poisonous relationships. Help me find the people and places where my light can shine.

Jesus, You promised the Advocate, the Comforter, to remain with me after You ascended into heaven. I recognize my need for the Holy Spirit. I simply cannot do this on my own. Spirit of God, breathe through my lungs. Form Your words on my lips. Give voice to the will of God. Help me know when and how to release others when it is within my power to do so.

Spoken in the Spirit through Jesus, the Son, to the Father. Amen.

CHAPTER 28

DIVINE MERCY

God is speaking to you. Listen!

My child, I am so happy that you are trying to walk the way revealed by My Son, Jesus. You hunger for His teaching. Bend your ear now and listen. If you wish to imitate Him in all things, then consider His mercy. Jesus could have come to earth with a sword to punish. Punishment was justified. Justice is to give someone what is owed to them. Instead of chastisement, Jesus showed compassion and forgiveness. This is mercy.

"Praise be to the God and Father of our Lord Jesus Christ! In his great mercy, he has given us new birth into a living hope through the resurrection of Jesus Christ from the dead" (1 Peter 1:3).

"But because of his great love for us, God, who is rich in mercy, made us alive with Christ even when we were dead in transgressions—it is by grace you have been saved" (Ephesians 2:4-5).

Justice demands giving someone what he or she deserves, what is their due. When one opens their heart to compassion for the offender and offers forgiveness and not justice, mercy is born. Mercy occurs when one acts on compassion.

Joseph's story in Genesis offers you an example of mercy as it challenges each individual to examine their own behavior. Joseph was the youngest of twelve brothers, and he was a dreamer. His own father was fascinated with the boy and favored him. The other brothers grew jealous and decided to murder Joseph. They threw him into a dry cistern to starve to death. Meanwhile, they saw a passing caravan and agreed that Joseph could be sold as a slave and make some profit. The brothers took Joseph's cloak, a special gift from their father, covered it in goat's blood, and brought it back to their father with news that his son was dead, killed by a wild beast. This horrifically cruel act was an act of revenge on their father for favoring Joseph.

Joseph's life following his sale into slavery became both a nightmare and a wonderful dream, for he experienced both deprivation and abundance, punishment and reward. His slavery eventually found him in prison, powerless, bound by irons, and unjustly accused of rape. He was brought out of prison to interpret a dream for Pharaoh and found favor. Pharaoh placed Joseph in the second most powerful position in the kingdom.

Meanwhile, Joseph's family in Hebron, the land of Canaan, faced starvation because of a drought. His brothers traveled to Egypt to purchase grain. Unknowing, they were brought before their brother, who was dressed in foreign garb and speaking Egyptian. They had no clue it was Joseph.

Justice called for their imprisonment and execution. Joseph forewent justice and chose compassion. He granted his brothers forgiveness, freedom, and grain. Joseph recognized that I, the God of Israel, used the evil intended by his brothers to do good, to save My people. All things work together for good for those who have faith.

Jesus' parable of the Prodigal Son is also a parable of My divine mercy. The younger son squandered his inheritance. The older son, who stayed home and labored on the Father's farm, wanted his brother treated like a servant. After all, the younger son had spent every cent of his inheritance, so he deserved nothing more. This is justice. Technically, the half of the estate that remained would be the elder brother's. Whatever the younger brother received now would be at the expense of the older brother.

The Father saw his younger son approaching and from a distance ran across the fields to greet him. He threw his arms around the young man, kissed him, and even before an apology could be offered, the father ordered a celebratory feast. The best robe they could find was put on the boy's shoulders, shoes were found for the barefoot beggar, and a valuable ring was placed on his finger. Forgiveness and compassion burst forth and materialized in acts of concrete love. Justice demanded the boy be cast out. Mercy cast justice aside and welcomed him home. Is this not the story of the Cross? I am the Father, and Jesus is My mercy. (Luke 15)

Jesus, My Son, is rejected, humiliated, spat on, cursed, tortured, and crucified. Justice demands I destroy those responsible. Jesus looks beyond the behavior of humanity and asks for mercy. "Father, forgive them, for they do not know what they are doing" (Luke 23:34). Keep in mind that those who actually murdered Jesus never offered any remorse. They were miserable, corrupt, and cruel. Jesus pities them in their diminished humanity. I am the Lord, your God. There is no other god. My mercy is vast and incomprehensible to all who do not know the Spirit.

If you are to walk in the steps of Jesus, you must love as Jesus loved, and Jesus loved with mercy. "As the body without the spirit is dead, so faith without deeds is dead" (James 2:26).

How might you imitate the mercy of Jesus? Illegal immigrants are pouring into your countries from foreign lands. They are consuming resources that could be spent on disadvantaged citizens. Some are raping and murdering your fellow countrymen who are footing the bill for all their meals, insurance, and living accommodations. Justice demands strangers leave your homeland. Mercy forgoes justice. A waitress is impolite and offers poor service. Justice calls for a complaint to the manager and a reduced tip. The person living with Christ leaves the restaurant having offered the expected tip without complaining to the manager. This is mercy.

You hear that a close friend has made some disparaging remarks about you. Justice demands confrontation and an apology. The mercy of Christ either makes an apology easier for the person who made the remarks or forgives the entire incident and never mentions it to the friend. A neighbor has erected a fence you know to be six inches over the property line. Justice insists the fence be moved. Mercy understands the financial strain of moving the fence and lets the fence stand.

G. K. Chesterton, a faithful disciple of Mine, once said that "The Christian idea has not been tried and found wanting. It has been found difficult and left untried."[2] It is easy to feel pity, compassion, and remorse. It is the Holy Spirit that takes the compassion and acts on it. This is mercy. This is Christ.

---

2   G. K. Chesterton, *What is Wrong with the World*

My Prayer

Jesus, hear my prayer. To be honest with You, Lord, I haven't thought much about mercy. The fact is I don't think I knew what it was before I read this book. I see the truth of it now. I see how the behavior of a Christian might stand apart from the behavior of those without Jesus. My behavior could be different. It makes me think of things happening right now in my own life, my country, and in the world. Yes, I understand that mercy is necessary, but like all Your teaching, the Spirit is given to discern courses of action that are multidimensional in their consequences. Unchecked migration could spell the end of Western civilization. Courses of action are not always clear.

How would mercy change what is going on between warring parties if they forgo justice? Those of us who proclaim Jesus as our personal Savior could really change the world if we opened our lives to Christ's divine mercy. I, as an individual, need to remind myself that an ocean is made of single drops of water. Jesus asks me to be concerned just with that one drop of water that is me.

Jesus, awaken my mind to opportunities for mercy. I need to stop jumping so quickly to demand justice and instead seek Jesus, who is in His flesh both love and mercy. Will some people take advantage and fail to thank me? Yes, they most certainly will. But taking each situation and offering it to Jesus, lifting it up for the Father's blessing as a sacrifice, opens the gates of heaven for the Holy Spirit to flood the earth. Mercy gives spiritual life to acts of kindness, charity, forgiveness, and even love.

I stand with Jesus and trust that people can change. Even the hardest among us can learn to love. Spirit of God, I know that if You can make a universe, it is a small task to make a new life for someone who is wretched. Father, pour Your Spirit upon this world and all its people. Pour Your Spirit into my heart and mind that I might truly become Christ for others. Jesus, live in me, speak through me, see with my eyes, and do the Father's work using my hands. All glory and praise to You, Lord Jesus Christ. Amen.

Spoken in the Spirit through Jesus, the Son, to the Father. Amen.

CHAPTER 29

I WILL GIVE YOU A NEW HEART

God is speaking to you. Listen!

"I will give you a new heart and put a new spirit in you; I will remove from you your heart of stone and give you a heart of flesh."

Ezekiel 36:26

Stony hearts—hearts hardened by indifference, apathy, and self-absorption—fail to awaken to My presence or to the humanity of one's brothers and sisters. A life lived with a heart of stone is a life on the periphery of what it could be, leaving good undone. It is a truly sad creature.

The Pharaoh of Egypt during Moses' time was a man with a heart of stone! He thought himself a god, a man above others. Born into privilege and power, he considered himself the source of wisdom. Deaf and blind to My Spirit, Pharaoh failed to see My children as human, equal to himself. He believed that the Jews, and even his own people, existed solely for his pleasure, service, and needs. His heart was more rigid than the stones of his pyramids.

Only those who have completely bolted the doors of their hearts against Me can be impervious to the suffering of others. Pharaoh is not alone in this world; he has many children today, people without compassion.

People often forget that Mary and Joseph were homeless refugees, illegal immigrants fleeing King Herod in search of safety, work, and welcome. You would think that Christians who know this would be moved by the tens of millions of their brothers and sisters who flee poverty, gangs, war, and the collapse of civil society. How could I not take indifference to the suffering of My children personally, when My own parents were immigrants in a foreign land and My people were slaves in Egypt? Now, do you see why the way you treat those without power is central to your final judgment? The disenfranchised are My family. "For I was hungry, and you gave me something to eat, I was thirsty, and you gave me something to drink, I was a stranger, and you invited me in, I needed clothes, and you clothed me, I was sick, and you looked after me, I was in prison, and you came to visit me" (Matthew 25:35-36). Hardened hearts!

Hearts have hardened to My commandments. "You shall not misuse the name of the LORD your God, for the LORD will not hold anyone guiltless who misuses His name" (Exodus 20:7). "Therefore God exalted Him to the highest place and gave Him the name that is above every name, that at the name of Jesus every knee should bow, in heaven and on earth and under the earth, and every tongue acknowledge that Jesus Christ is Lord, to the glory of God the Father" (Philippians 2:9-11). My most precious gift is Jesus, My Son. At His name, every knee in heaven bends, every head should bow. Yet, His name is trivialized and emptied as it is spoken on your TV programs with indifference. This sacrilege passes without comment. The use of My name in the media is a well-thought-out and calculated act to normalize sacrilege and breed contempt for the Christian way. No shock or revulsion courses through your veins at the offense. Hardened hearts!

I see your hearts of stone. Yet I wait. One day passes, and then another. And another. I am not willing to give up on you or on humanity. Where are your acts of charity and mercy? "Come near to God and he will come near to you. Wash your hands, you sinners, and purify your hearts, you double-minded" (James 4:8). My child, "Create in me a pure heart, O God, and renew a steadfast spirit within me" (Psalm 51:10), and I will make it new again. I will knead your heart like dough. It will warm in My hands, reshape in My care. I will roll it out to make you into bread for this world. "The LORD is close to the brokenhearted and saves those who are crushed in spirit" (Psalm 34:18). I will give you a new heart, sew a new spirit within you. I will heal you of your blindness, and you will awaken from this sleep.

The signs of My love and care abound. Open your hearts to Me! I am here. "Come to me, all you who are weary and burdened, and I will give you rest. Take my yoke upon you and learn from me, for I am gentle and humble in heart, and you will find rest for your souls" (Matthew 11:28-29).

My Prayer

Lord of mercy. "I will give thanks to You, LORD, with all my heart" (Psalm 9:1). I have been blessed in every way. I have been blessed by You, Father-Creator; Jesus, Lamb of God; You, Holy Spirit, breath of heaven. Break my heart of stone! Let compassion, mercy, charity, empathy, and a commitment to work for a better world come forth. I am like Pharaoh in that sometimes my own interests are all that consume me. There are times when I lose myself in my own needs and my world collapses into me, myself, and mine.

Father, let my gratitude for my unearned blessings motivate me to seek ways I might become a blessing to others. I did not merit my birth or opportunities: the parents You chose for me, the century into which I was born, the food and medical care I am privileged to enjoy. Help me to seek the well-being of others. Let me become one with Jesus and His body on earth, reaching out in compassion to lift the burdens that weigh down humankind.

"He does not treat us as our sins deserve or repay us according to our iniquities. For as high as the heavens are above the earth, so great is his love for those who fear him" (Psalm 103:10-11).

Jesus, I lived inside a delusion, a false universe, a lie. I thought it was my strength that sustained me, not Yours! I was vain and thought myself the author of my own life. I used to think it was my work, my sacrifice, my treasure, my abilities, and my choices alone that brought blessings into my life. I had done no "bad" things for which I should be ashamed. I had no sin.

Little did I realize that sin is not necessarily what one does, but what one leaves undone. Sin is what I become when I refuse communion with You, my Lord and God, and communion with others. Forgive me for my sin, my indifference, and my self-centered attribution of power to myself when I am nothing without You, Lord. You are the source of every good thing I have ever been privileged to enjoy.

I have stood in pride within my self-made universe, and it is here, against all reason, that You look upon me now with Your divine mercy. You give Yourself to me. You touch my eyes with the breath of Your Spirit and make me see. You unveil the truth of who I am and show me, through Christ, who I might become. I am no more than dust. I am a mist that burns away in the morning sun. I am the blade of grass that withers in the desert. I cried out, "Examine my heart and my mind" (Psalm 26:2), and You did more than examine. You made something new inside me. You created a new heart and a new spirit within me.

Jesus, take my heart of stone. Give me a new heart. Give birth within me to Your compassion. Put prophecy in my mind. Use me according to Your holy will. Fulfill Your promise: "I will give you a new heart and put a new spirit in you; I will remove from you your heart of stone and give you a heart of flesh" (Ezekiel 36:26). Mercy. Lord Jesus, have mercy on me, a sinner.

Jesus, I pledge to love You, Lord, with all my heart and with all my soul and with all my mind (Matthew 22:37). I will trust in You, Lord, with my life and no longer lean on my own understanding (Proverbs 3:5). You, Lord, "are the strength of my heart" (Psalm 73:26). "I give thanks to you, LORD, with all my heart; I will tell of all your wonderful deeds" (Psalm 9:1). "Create in me a pure heart, O God, and renew a steadfast spirit within me" (Psalm 51:10). You, Lord God, are a "consuming fire" (Hebrews 12:29), and I beg You to teach me, Holy Spirit. Teach me all things and never tire of reminding me of Jesus' way to guide my steps and make decisions (John 14:26). Speak to me, Jesus, and may Your word burn in my heart as it did for the disciples You walked with on the road to Emmaus. Open the Scriptures to me, Lord (Luke 24:32).

Measure my love for You, Lord, with the measure I use to become a blessing to others. I will work to see that the homeless find shelter, those who live in fear find safety, and minister to the hungry and imprisoned. Help me to sympathize with the desperation that leads to theft and the hopelessness that leads to people selling themselves to feed their children. I will vote for people who will serve the needs of those with no power.

Glory to You, image of the invisible God, Word through whom all things have come into being, Lord Jesus Christ. You are the Lamb that was slain. It is Your blood poured over my heart that makes me clean and heals me. Touch the eyes of my heart, Jesus, and help me to see again.

Spoken in the Spirit through Jesus, the Son, to the Father. Amen.

CHAPTER 30

HELP WHEN YOU ARE DESPERATE

God is speaking to you. Listen!

My child, today I have a message for that moment in your life you would describe using a word beginning with the letter D: Desperate. Dejected. Dismissed as if you were a piece of garbage. Depleted, run out, empty. One day you may find yourself wondering if there is any hope for your situation. You may think there is no way forward, no way out of a bad situation.

Elijah's story in Scripture is one of desperation. "Elijah was afraid and ran for his life. When he came to Beersheba in Judah, he left his servant there, while he himself went a day's journey into the wilderness. He came to a broom bush, sat down under it, and prayed that he might die. 'I have had enough, LORD,' he said. 'Take my life; I am no better than my ancestors.' Then he lay down under the bush and fell asleep. All at once an angel touched him and said, 'Get up and eat'" (1 Kings 19:3-5).

Elijah did everything I asked, yet his predicament worsened as he followed My lead. He finally reached a critical point in his journey, thinking he just couldn't go on any longer, either physically or emotionally. It was a dead end. Queen Jezebel had put out an order for Elijah's death, so he was being pursued. Everyone had turned on him. There was no help anywhere from anyone. He fled into the wilderness, sat down, and realized he was finished. No more plans. No more resources. No more energy or motivation. He could not take even one more step on his own. Elijah prayed to die. He had had enough of living.

An angel appeared at his side and spoke: "Get up and eat." Notice that the angel began no long discourse on why Elijah should reengage with life. The angel offered no advice on how to better handle his problems. No promise of friends waiting to help out. No pep talk on positive thinking. No prophecy that the next Powerball had his name on it. Just one simple movement of his body. That was all the angel asked.

"Sit up, Elijah, so you don't choke. Look for the piece of bread. Stretch out your arm. Break off just one little piece. Put it in your mouth. Chew. Swallow. Wait and repeat. Get up and eat!"

When you are desperate, you need to stop thinking about who or what forced you into the desert, what hammered you into the ground. When you despair, you need to forget about everything and everyone in the whole world and just concentrate on breathing. That's it. Just breathe. If you can do just that, there is hope. You are still alive. You can make choices. The only choice you have to make is very tiny, but difficult: sit up so you don't choke. Look for the bread. Stretch out your arm. Break off a little piece of bread. Eat.

Desperation calls for little steps, insignificant movements that shut down all the voices in the universe except that one voice speaking in your heart. It is the voice of an angel, yes, but for you as a follower of Jesus, it is not an angel, but rather the Holy Spirit. The Spirit was Jesus' gift to you when you first came to believe. "Never will I leave you; never will I forsake you" (Hebrews 13:5). "And surely I am with you always, to the very end of the age" (Matthew 28:20).

After Elijah ate, he was instructed to listen for Me, the Lord God, for I was waiting to speak with him. Elijah tried to listen, but he still couldn't hear My voice. There were still too many echoes bouncing back and forth in his brain from his wretched experiences in the world. It would take time. I would not give up. I kept speaking. Elijah thought I might be speaking in the strong and heavy wind that crushes rocks. I was not speaking in the mighty wind. Then he thought he heard My voice in an earthquake. I was not in the earthquake. He thought it was Me speaking in a fire. No. It was not My voice. Finally, Elijah recognized My voice in a tiny whisper.

So, what is My lesson to you who are desperate and want to give up? First, shut off every voice in your head. Stop thinking about your problem or its solution. Stop listening to the voices that are pursuing you, condemning or cursing you, criticizing you, or even the voices offering you advice. Don't bother blaming someone else for getting you here.

Second, think of one tiny movement you know you can pull off. This tiny step might be to go home and lie down for a nap. It might be to call off work tomorrow, claiming sickness. Have a glass of wine. Eat some ice cream. Third, name the lie that you are alone. That will never be true for a follower of Jesus. I sent My own Spirit to dwell within you, so how could you even think of yourself as alone? I will be with you always. Fourth, listen for My whisper. I will always be your shepherd and guide. You don't need to solve the problems of the world; just take one step at a time, careful to observe all Jesus taught you.

My Holy Spirit has the plan, but the Spirit will only tell you where to place your next step, not plan out your year. One step. One little task to move you forward. You can do it. Sit up and eat, but not really. That line is simply a message for you to do something small. After you accomplish that one small task, just listen for My whisper. I will not abandon you. I will simply tell you where to place your next step.

The present message for desperate times is also a message found in two words in the prayer Jesus, My Son, taught you: daily bread. Give us today our daily bread. One day's problems are enough. Not the whole year or even the week. One day at a time. Today. Not the past. Not the future. Today. Present tense. "Therefore do not worry about tomorrow, for tomorrow will worry about itself. Each day has enough trouble of its own" (Matthew 6:34).

Today, I am speaking in a whisper, and you need to call your mind back from the past and pull it in from the future to hear Me speak in the present. If you draw yourself into the present moment, you will be available to hear My voice. I will never ask too much of you. If you stay with Me in the present moment and just do one little thing, we will build a pyramid together. We will move a mountain. We will make you into the body of Christ, and you will share in My glory. My plan isn't for you to be a success in this world. This world is passing away. My plan is for you to dwell within My heavenly kingdom! Get up and eat!

My Prayer

Jesus, You are my Savior. I guess, in a way, I might need to experience some sort of cataclysmic event to put me in a place where I am completely stripped of my defenses and open to Your word. Would a letter of rejection or a task that stands beyond my talents or abilities do the trick? A traumatic event, sudden death, or terminal disease? What could empty me like Elijah the prophet was emptied in order to hear Your whisper?

Bring me to lay beside Elijah in the wilderness. Help me to give up relying on my own resources and begin relying totally on You. Come, Spirit of God, and be my daily bread. Help me decide what keys to press on the computer, what prayers to say, what people to contact, what step to take forward. Let me pull my life back from the past and future to stand in the present before You.

Lamb of God, You sit on the mighty throne in the center of the cosmos and bend Your ear to hear my voice. Thank You, mighty King. May I never forget that ultimately You have all power. You are in control. You set boundaries for the sea and the sun. Nothing can happen that is not permitted by You, and no event exists beyond Your ability to use it for good. You take every situation and command that good somehow be born from it. You take every trial and make me strong, every defeat and turn it into victory in preparation for Your kingdom. Let every step I take, every morsel of bread I eat, lead me closer and closer to You, Lamb that was slain.

Jesus, this talk of desperation reminds me of Hannah's experience recounted in the Old Testament. Hannah was desperate for a child. She went to You in utter anguish of spirit and spoke to You from her sorrowful heart. The world had beaten her down. Ridicule. Barrenness. A life stripped of meaning. She saw no hope. She voiced her grief, her lost dream. She lamented that she would never be called "mother." Hannah poured her soul out in misery before You, just as Your priests poured the sacrificed blood upon the temple altar. You bent to wipe her tears and picked her up. You were her hope and salvation (1 Samuel 1-2).

"Yes, my soul, find rest in God; my hope comes from him. Truly he is my rock and my salvation; he is my fortress, I will not be shaken. . . . Trust in him at all times, you people; pour out your hearts to him, for God is our refuge" (Psalm 62:5-6, 8).

Open my ears, Lord, so that the first whisper I hear through the silence is Your voice. Speak words of healing over my broken spirit. Raise my face from the sands of the earth that I might see You, my Redeemer, my Savior. Hold out Your love, kindness, and compassion to me and say, "Take and eat." Where does my strength come from? It comes from the Lord God, the Almighty. It comes from You, Holy Spirit. You are my daily bread, the cup that does not run dry.

"I love you, LORD, my strength. The LORD is my rock, my fortress, and my deliverer; my God is my rock, in whom I take refuge, my shield and the horn of my salvation, my stronghold. I called to the LORD, who is worthy of praise, and I have been saved from my enemies. . . . In my distress, I called to the LORD; I cried to my God for help. From his temple he heard my voice; my cry came before him, into his ears" (Psalm 18:1-3, 6).

All glory to You, Lord Jesus Christ. Amen.

Spoken in the Spirit, through Jesus, the Son, to the Father. Amen.

CHAPTER 31

GOD WILL STAND GUARD OVER YOU

God is speaking to you. Listen!

My dear child, listen to Me. You don't have to fight any battle on your own. Remember, I told you that I will guard you. I am your protector.

"I lift up my eyes to the mountains—where does my help come from? My help comes from the LORD, the Maker of heaven and earth. He will not let your foot slip—he who watches over you will not slumber; indeed, he who watches over Israel will neither slumber nor sleep. The LORD watches over you—the LORD is your shade at your right hand; the sun will not harm you by day, nor the moon by night. The LORD will keep you from all harm—he will watch over your life; the LORD will watch over your coming and going both now and forevermore."

Psalm 121:1-8

My children, why do you choose to live in fear when I have promised to guard you? Listen to the psalmist. I inspired these words for your sake. I watch over you to protect you from harm. Your life is truly in the palm of My hand. No evil can befall you unless I permit it, and if I do permit it, there is a reason.

Learn of My protection from the story of Joseph, the son of Jacob. He was thrown into a cistern to starve, sold into slavery, and chained with irons in prison, all because his brothers acted against him. When Joseph finally reflected on all the bad things that had happened to him, he said to his brothers, "You intended to harm me, but God intended it for good to accomplish what is now being done, the saving of many lives" (Genesis 50:20). I, your Lord, always bring good forth from evil. Pray "Thy will be done" and then leave your life in My care, under My providence. Trust Me.

"Rejoice in the Lord always. I will say it again: Rejoice! Let your gentleness be evident to all. The Lord is near. Do not be anxious about anything, but in every situation, by prayer and petition, with thanksgiving, present your requests to God. And the peace of God, which transcends all understanding, will guard your hearts and your minds in Christ Jesus."

Philippians 4:4-7

Believe these words. They are St. Paul's words. They are My words. Remind yourself that you are not alone. Articulate your fear in a prayer. Then give Me your fear. Trust Me to take the situation under My control and to protect you.

If you are about to go in for surgery, imagine the stretcher beneath you is My hand. I am holding you in the palm of My hand (Isaiah 49:16). Close your eyes and imagine it is I who wheel you into surgery. As you are anesthetized, I am guarding the hand of the anesthesiologist and monitoring your heartbeat. As you are being cut open, I am guiding the doctor's hand. I am checking for bleeding. I am watching for bacteria and viruses in the air and on medical instruments. Using the imagination I gave you, pray not just during surgery, but in every circumstance where you experience anxiety or fear.

I set the sky above the earth's atmosphere to shield and protect you from harmful radiation from the sun. If I can do this on a planetary scale, why would I not protect one of My children in their daily comings and goings? Know that I am your shield, your refuge from danger (Psalm 18:30). I am your rock, your deliverer who watches over you day and night (Psalm 18:2).

Imagine a mother bird extending her wings over her chicks to keep them warm. I cover you with My protection and under My wings, I provide you with refuge. I am guarding you right now in this moment from all predators and from evil (2 Thessalonians 3:3). "So do not fear, for I am with you; do not be dismayed, for I am your God. I will strengthen you and help you; I will uphold you with my righteous right hand" (Isaiah 41:10).

My Prayer

"I call out to the LORD, and he answers me from his holy mountain. . . From the LORD comes deliverance. May your blessing be on your people" (Psalm 3:4, 8). "In peace I will

lie down and sleep, for you alone, LORD, make me dwell in safety" (Psalm 4:8).

"Be strong and courageous. Do not be afraid or terrified because of them, for the LORD your God goes with you; He will never leave you nor forsake you" (Deuteronomy 31:6).

Jesus, Lord, I am anxious and frightened. I feel danger. I sense in my bones that something bad is going to happen. It may happen to me, or even worse, to someone I love. I feel danger drawing closer. I know it yearns to destroy the peace, health, relationships, or security, either for myself or a loved one. I hear an unjust accusation of some misdeed that never occurred. I feel an enemy about to threaten a marriage, harm the young in my family, or disrupt our country. I have a premonition that something bad is going to happen. I smell it. I feel it in my bones.

I wonder if the closer I draw to You, Lord Jesus, the more intense the danger of something bad happening becomes. Our relationship threatens the forces of this world, and so they watch for an opportunity to devastate and bring ruin to my life or those I love. Jesus, You have gifted me with a happy family. Please guard and protect this sacred and holy gift. I declare Your protection over those I love. I invoke Your promise of aid in times of tribulation. I place myself within the walls of Your temple and ask for the prayers of the community of believers here on earth and before Your throne in heaven.

Sometimes, despite Your support and fidelity, Father, against all reason, I just feel alone. I wonder if I am strong enough to face the future with all that might go wrong. I try to remind myself that "My flesh and my heart may fail, but God is the strength of my heart and my portion forever"

(Psalm 73:26). Sustain me in my efforts to be a faithful and true disciple.

I am afraid I can't be as strong as those Christians who came before me. I don't possibly measure up to the level of trust I find in Paul's letters. "We are hard-pressed on every side, but not crushed; perplexed, but not in despair; persecuted, but not abandoned; struck down, but not destroyed. We always carry around in our body the death of Jesus so that the life of Jesus may also be revealed in our body" (2 Corinthians 4:8-10).

The Christians mentioned in this scripture were all treasures in earthen vessels, for it was Your power within them that made living like Jesus possible. They were so brave. They knew the Holy Spirit, not just as individuals but as a community. Together they called out, and You heard. They felt Your power. They rejoiced in Your glory. I feel like I always come up short on faith, on trust, and on my ability to persevere. Help me to believe in You, Lord, and also to believe in myself.

I reach out to You now, Jesus, and ask that I might stand one day with Your holy ones in heaven, Your saints. I ask their intercession as I ask for the prayers of all the living. The saints claimed You as Savior and stood in Your power. Your Word is mighty. Your love is everlasting. I belong to You, Jesus. Lord, guard those I love, my family and friends. Protect us from evil and sustain us in trial. Give us our daily bread and deliver us from evil.

"Though the LORD is exalted, he looks kindly on the lowly; though lofty, he sees them from afar. Though I walk in the midst of trouble, you preserve my life. You stretch out your hand against the anger of my foes; with your right hand you save me. The LORD will vindicate me; Your love,

LORD, endures forever—do not abandon the works of your hands" (Psalm 138:6-8).

"I cry out to God Most High, to God, who vindicates me. He sends from heaven and saves me, rebuking those who hotly pursue me—God sends forth his love and his faithfulness. I am in the midst of lions; I am forced to dwell among ravenous beasts—men whose teeth are spears and arrows, whose tongues are sharp swords" (Psalm 57:2-4).

You foresaw my tribulation, Lord Jesus. You prayed to the Father that I and my loved ones might never perish, that no power might snatch us out of Your hand. The Father gave us to You, Jesus, and no one can snatch us out of Your wounded hand. You and the Father are One! (John 10:28-30). How could I allow my fear to bring me so low as to doubt Your mighty power? You are the Creator, O Lord, and all spirits are creatures subject to Your power.

The battle between evil and You, Lord, was never a true battle, for You are God, and there is no one before You! Lord, You cannot be threatened by a creature. Evil is nothing more or less than a creature. You are Creator. All I need to do is look to You, Lord God, King, Victor-Triumphant. I choose to stand before You, Almighty God, guardian of Your people. No evil dares enter Your courts. No wolf dares threaten Your sheep. You are the good shepherd. You, God of Israel, will guard me and those I love. You have spoken. And so, it will be as You declare.

"The LORD is my shepherd, I lack nothing. He makes me lie down in green pastures; he leads me beside quiet waters, he refreshes my soul. He guides me along the right paths for his name's sake. Even though I walk through the darkest valley, I will fear no evil, for you are with me; your rod and your staff, they comfort me. You prepare a table before me *in the presence of my enemies. You anoint my head with oil; my cup overflows. Surely your goodness and love will follow me all the days of my life, and I will dwell in the house of the LORD forever" (Psalm 23).*

Glory to You, Word of God, Lord Jesus Christ. Amen.

Spoken in the Spirit through Jesus, the Son, to the Father. Amen.

CHAPTER 32

ASHAMED TO SPEAK OF JESUS

God is speaking to you. Listen!

My child, I am glad you are here. Let Me ask you—
have you ever been hesitant to let others know
how much you love Me?

"Whoever acknowledges me before others, I will also acknowledge before my Father in heaven" (Matthew 10:32).
Reflect on this: sometimes, people feel ashamed of their her-
itage or background. Children of immigrants, for instance,
might have refused to speak their native language at school,
hoping to fit in. They felt embarrassed to be different. Even
adults might feel ashamed of their parents' struggles or challenges, hiding the truth to protect themselves from judgment. Imagine the Boy Scout who, instead of admitting "My
Dad is home drunk," says, "He had to work," to avoid shame.

In the same way, many Christians feel hesitant to make their
faith in Me, your Savior Jesus, known. They may bow their
heads to pray at home but hesitate to do so in public, especially at gatherings with coworkers, friends, or even ex-
tended family. They might worry about making others feel

"uncomfortable." But reflect on this: the feelings of others are often placed above reverence for the Creator of all. My disciples miss the opportunity to remind their brothers and sisters of the true source of the blessings they enjoy, including the food they share—Me.

Today, many are ashamed to be associated with the church due to well-publicized scandals. They lack a deep understanding of their faith, and without this knowledge, they find it easy to distance themselves from organized religion. They see the church through the lens of media portrayals— corrupt, hypocritical, and filled with hatred. Among "intellectuals," atheism is often seen as a sign of being well-read and introspective. Students worry that professing their faith could affect their grades, fearing that a professor might look down on them for being a serious Christian.

"Whoever is ashamed of me and of my words, the Son of Man will be ashamed of them when he comes in his glory and in the glory of the Father and of the holy angels" (Luke 9:26). "Here is a trust worthy saying: If we have died with him, we will also live with him; if we endure, we will also reign with him. If we disown him, He will also disown us" (2 Timothy 2:11-12). Reflect on this truth: if I am not accepted as Lord and Savior, I will honor that decision in the hereafter. Why would I force someone to live in a kingdom they don't believe in, with a God they don't accept? "Then he will say to those on his left, 'Depart from me, you who are cursed, into the eternal fire prepared for the devil and his angels'" (Matthew 25:41).

I am Jesus, and being denied is not foreign to Me. Peter, who lived with Me for three years, night and day, who witnessed My miracles, still denied Me. He thought it impossible when I first told him, saying, "Even if all fall away, I will not" (Mark 14:29). Yet three times he denied knowing who I was.

I forgave Peter because his denial occurred before My resurrection and the coming of the Holy Spirit. But now, you have received the Holy Spirit, who has brought you into My inner circle, My family, My body. To deny Me now, after knowing I am the Living Word, the Creator, the Good Shepherd, the Savior, is a grave offense. Reflect on this: denial now is a monstrous insult to all I Am and all I have given you. You cannot desecrate a temple from the outside—true desecration happens within. The Holy Spirit has brought you into the temple sanctuary. To deny Me now is desecration and sacrilege. You know My Name, you have shared in My sacrifice, and yet, to deny Me—how is this even possible?

"At the name of Jesus every knee should bow, in heaven and on earth and under the earth, and every tongue acknowledge that Jesus Christ is Lord, to the glory of God the Father" (Philippians 2:10-11). Reflect on this: why would any true Christian be ashamed? If the Holy Spirit truly lives within you, you should be shouting My name from the rooftops! My life, death, and resurrection are Good News. Why would you hide a precious gem? You would naturally want to wear it, to let others see its beauty. My gospel is not just any treasure—it is the only treasure that brings eternal life.

No, all religions are not the same! I am the Lord God, and there is no other. Reflect on this: faith in Jesus is not just one option among many; it is the truth that leads to salvation. This world is passing away, and if you believe this, you are morally and ethically bound to share the news of Jesus with everyone. The boat is sinking, and you have the key to the life raft. You have an obligation to share the Word of Christ.

All Christians bear the responsibility of witnessing about Me as Lord and Savior. Every opportunity should be seized to make it known that I, the living God, have changed your life and that I am love. Before I ascended to heaven, I commissioned not just the apostles but all who would follow in the Holy Spirit. Reflect on My last words before returning to the Father: "All authority in heaven and on earth has been given to Me. Therefore go and make disciples of all nations, baptizing them in the name of the Father and of the Son and of the Holy Spirit, and teaching them to obey everything I have commanded you. And surely I am with you always, to the very end of the age" (Matthew 28:18-20).

My Prayer

Jesus, I am sorry. It is true—I didn't fully realize what was happening. There have been times when I was not proud to be a Christian. I let the media shape and control my thoughts and behavior instead of You. I should have seen through the manipulation. There have been billions of Christians over the last 2,000 years, and it's easy to find monsters among them in every age and denomination. Even today, with millions of pastors around the world, there is no shortage of horrific stories involving church leaders that dominate the news. But I should have found peace in the truth that these monsters are a minority and that most of Your servants are righteous and honest people. I have been manipulated. I should be proud of the Christian church and its servants who are good.

The world is being led to believe that Christians are not good people, but the truth is that goodness abounds among those who are faithful to Jesus. Help me to be a witness to that goodness and to celebrate the wonderful work of Christians everywhere. The message of Jesus and His church has changed human history for the better! Help me never to be ashamed of Your people, Lord.

My shame is a scandal. My hesitation to admit I am part of Your people has compromised my commitment to serve You, Jesus. I have allowed myself to be influenced by the accuser's lies. It is I whom You are speaking to in Revelation 3:15-16: "I know your deeds, that you are neither cold nor hot. I wish you were either one or the other! So, because you are lukewarm—neither hot nor cold—I am about to spit you out of my mouth." I have been a lukewarm Christian, trying to play both sides, not standing firm in my loyalty to Christ, the true witness, and source of the Father's creation.

Jesus, You are my Lord and Savior. You are the Word who made the universe, and You made me. You came to earth, suffered, and died so that I might be forgiven for my sins. You opened the gates of heaven. You promised to come back and take me with You. Jesus, You are worthy of all praise and glory. Let me boldly witness my faith in You.

Jesus, I stand with St. Paul and, with You as my witness, proclaim, "For I am not ashamed of the gospel, because it is the power of God that brings salvation to everyone who believes" (Romans 1:16).

Holy Spirit, renew Your life within me. Clear my head of all false thoughts and help me to focus on the gift that is Jesus and the gospel. Help me in every time and place to boldly and proudly witness my faith in Jesus. Give me courage, Lord. Never let me cower or hesitate to give witness.

Holy Spirit, open my lips that I may boast of Jesus and the power of the cross. Let me give testimony to how Jesus has changed my life, opened my heart, and lifted me from despair. Holy Spirit, lead me in wisdom and continue to reveal to me the way of Jesus. Watch over my steps so that I might always be directed toward Your kingdom. Be my strength and empower me to serve the Lord.

Jesus, there is a battle going on for the hearts and minds of our young and our old. May Your Spirit lift up Your church, the body of Christ, throughout the world to speak the truth of Jesus. May all denominations within Your one church, Your body, support and encourage one another. May every Christian fellowship see the good in every other fellowship and name it to their members. "For whoever is not against us is for us" (Mark 9:40). May Your Word go out to all the earth and subdue it in the name of Jesus.

Jesus, renew Your Spirit within all parts of Your body on earth, and let us boldly proclaim You as Messiah.

"Great and marvelous are your deeds, Lord God Almighty. Just and true are your ways, King of the nations. Who will not fear You, Lord, and bring glory to Your name? For You alone are holy. All nations will come and worship before You, for Your righteous acts have been revealed" (Revelation 15:3b-4).

Spoken in the Spirit through Jesus, the Son, to the Father. Amen.

CHAPTER 33

BUT THEY DOUBTED

God is speaking to you. Listen!

"Then the eleven disciples went to Galilee, to the mountain where Jesus had told them to go. When they saw him, they worshiped him; but some doubted."

Matthew 28:16-17

Reflect on this: the eleven apostles who remained faithful to Me were ordinary human beings, just like you. They were not saints from the beginning; they were flawed, with weaknesses and fears. That is why you find these pillars of the church squabbling over who is the greatest, feeling defeated after unsuccessful missions, hiding on the night of My arrest, and even denying Me. They all had issues. James and John were called Sons of Thunder, not just for their tempers but for their pride and ambition (Mark 10:37). They were, in many ways, like you—imperfect and in need of grace.

These ordinary men witnessed My miracles, My crucifixion and My resurrection. Reflect on the moment I quoted at the beginning of this teaching from Matthew's Gospel. These words were spoken after My resurrection. The timing is important because at this point the apostles know that I am not just another man but the Son of God. They knew that the Father and I are one—I, Jesus, am equal to the Father in heaven. I am God! They know this because they have been baptized in the Spirit at Pentecost. The object of worship for the Jewish people was always and only God. Yet, despite all they had witnessed and experienced, even at My parting earthly life at the ascension, some of them still doubted.

But how did I respond to their doubt? I did not condemn their weak faith. I did not even draw attention to their doubt. Instead, I completely ignored it and proceeded to commission them to go out into the world and make disciples, baptizing them and teaching them to observe all that I had commanded.

Reflect on this: I called human beings to follow Me, not perfect beings or robots. Human beings are imperfect, fickle, and complex creatures, equipped with minds designed to question and evaluate. You are not a machine; your brain cannot simply turn off, even in sleep. Humans are, by design, capable of doubt. I made you this way, and doubt is a crucial part of critical thinking and survival. So why would I ever be repelled by or taken aback by doubt? When I recognized the doubt in My disciples, I moved closer to them. I did not chastise them; instead, I commissioned them. Reflect on this truth: My kingdom is bigger than human anxiety, fear, and even doubt.

By agreeing to follow Me, these eleven men—and by inclusion, you who are reading this now—did not commit to turning off their minds. You will continue to experience doubt at various times and intensities. What matters most is not that you have doubts but what you choose to believe despite them. Reflect on this: belief is a choice, a commitment to live in this world according to My Way. Belief is choosing to trust that I Am at your side, even when you don't feel My presence. Belief is choosing to stand in My goodness and light, even when you are facing immense suffering or evil.

Come, walk with Me through My garden. I call you My friend. I want you by My side just as you are, with all your imperfections. I will not give up on you just because you are having a bad day or are struggling with doubt. So, please, stop being anxious. Choose to believe that I will always, always love you. Believe it because it is true.

My Prayer

Jesus, help me overcome my doubt with stronger belief. I do not have the benefit of seeing You face to face as the apostles did in the upper room. Yet, despite not seeing You, despite my unbelief, keep me steadfast in my choice to believe. Walk with me each step of this journey so that I might keep the commandments and live according to Your teaching. Give me Your gift of peace, the peace that the world cannot give. Breathe Your Spirit into me every moment of every day. You are my Lord and my God. I worship You as the Lamb that was slain. I know that You are the Son of God. Grant me confidence in Your name, and help me to be a faithful and true witness.

As I walk through life with my doubts, I pledge, Jesus, that I will strive to be patient, kind, and forgiving. I will make a concerted effort each day to see the good in every person I encounter. Remind me to thank the store clerk for their help. Remind me to pray for the driver who honks at me, the coworker who cuts me down, and the fellow parishioner who acts uncharitably. Move me to offer compliments that might brighten someone's day. Let me build up the people I meet so they may be better for having met me. Help me to remember to raise my voice constantly in prayer.

Help me to have a listening heart and to truly empathize with those who trust me with pieces of their private stories. Alert me when I start to judge others, and help me know when it is time to be silent. Let me not be a stumbling block or a hindrance to anyone's journey toward You, Lord.

I remember how Peter tried to walk on water but was frightened by the wind and the waves. He faltered and began to sink. Reflecting on this, I pray, Lord, that when I feel overwhelmed and frightened by the storms of my life, You will stretch out Your hand and lift me up, just as You lifted Peter. Don't let the world win, Lord. Save me.

When I feel defeated, I tend to doubt, so I ask in advance for Your encouragement. Strengthen me when I am weak and want to give up. Give me the right words to say that I might bring people closer to Your kingdom and not speak foolishly. Let my prayers be offered with a clear heart, free from negative emotions or doubts, focused entirely on You.

May I never be ashamed to pray spontaneously, even in public. "For the Spirit God gave us does not make us timid, but gives us power, love, and self-discipline" (2 Timothy 1:7). Help me to stand strong in Your strength.

Spirit of Jesus, thank You for those moments when You encourage me to embrace Your power and let the fear caused by doubt diminish. Send me a friend when others abandon *or reject me. Renew my faith when I give in to fear. "The LORD is my light and my salvation—whom shall I fear? The LORD is the stronghold of my life—of whom shall I be afraid?" (Psalm 27:1).*

Holy Spirit, I pray that despite having doubts, I may never waver in my choice to follow Christ and to live His teaching. Jesus said, "Truly I tell you, if you have faith and do not doubt, not only can you do what was done to the fig tree, but also you can say to this mountain, 'Go, throw yourself into the sea,' and it will be done. If you believe, you will receive whatever you ask for in prayer" (Matthew 21:21-22).

Lord, I commit myself once again to keep Your commandments. Keep me faithful until I take my last breath. I choose to believe despite my unbelief. I choose to walk in Your steps and profess faith in our loving Father and in You through the Spirit.

Hand me a shield and armor so that I may fight the temptation to doubt, instigated by the prince of this world (Ephesians 6:16). Let the Holy Spirit be my spiritual armor. Make my faith like steel, a shield that can protect me from doubt.

Spirit, I know You choose when and how to answer my prayers. When I question why I don't see those prayers answered, remind me that You can bring forth good even from difficult situations. I am not privy to Your great plan, so make me patient and faithful as I surrender all my prayers to Your will. Strengthen my belief that You always hear and answer me. If I have a moment of fragility, let me hear Your voice echoing from the prophet Isaiah, "So do not fear, for I am with you; do not be dismayed, for I am your God. I will strengthen you and help you; I will uphold you with My righteous right hand" (Isaiah 41:10).

All glory to You, Lord Jesus Christ, Son of the living God, Redeemer of the world. Amen.

Spoken in the Spirit, through Jesus, the Son, to the Father. Amen.

CHAPTER 34

DRINK THE LIVING WATER

God is speaking to you. Listen!

The Grand Canyon, a majestic testament to the power of nature, stretches 277 miles long and plunges to depths of 6,000 feet. At its widest, it spans 15 miles. I carved this canyon deep into the Colorado plateau with water—living water. In the Bible, "living water" is also translated as "flowing water," and like the water that carved this vast canyon, the Spirit of Jesus moves with a power beyond comprehension. Reflect on this: water, which can cut through rock, tear down, and reshape landscapes, can also spring forth from the desert sands as a tiny stream, bringing life and hope to barren places. This metaphor captures the immense and indescribable power of My Spirit, the Spirit of Jesus, who is the Word that brought the cosmos into existence and sustains it still.

When Jesus spoke to the Samaritan woman at the well, He offered her living water—something far beyond the physical water she sought. "If you knew the gift of God and who it is that asks you for a drink, you would have asked him, and he would have given you living water" (John 4:10). My

Son offered her the Holy Spirit, the source of all spiritual life. Reflect on this gift: the Spirit has the power to create, cleanse, renew, give life, forgive, heal, comfort, protect, and nurture. This Spirit, which Jesus alone can provide, is what every human heart longs for—a thirst that only He can quench.

"Jesus stood and said in a loud voice, 'Let anyone who is thirsty come to me and drink. Whoever believes in me, as Scripture has said, rivers of living water will flow from within them.' By this he meant the Spirit, whom those who believed in him were later to receive" (John 7:37-39).

The living water of My Holy Spirit is meant to flow from within you, reshaping and healing the world around you. My Spirit has the power to dismantle the demonic patterns of thought and behavior that corrupt society and cause suffering. A blanket of darkness has descended over the earth, blinding humanity to truth and goodness. But it is through the rushing waters of Jesus's Spirit within you that the world can find redemption. Nothing can stand in the way of this living water. It humbles the proud, lifts up the lowly, and washes away the obstacles that Satan has placed to deceive and control. Reflect on the darkness that covers the earth, where good is seen as evil, and falsehood is accepted as truth. Only My Spirit can heal this blindness and restore wholeness.

My child, listen and understand that you are truly My legs, My hands, My voice in this world. The living water within you must flow from your life into the world. You are the light of the world, the salt of the earth, the Bride, the chosen and predestined, My son and My daughter! The living water is the Spirit of Christ living within you. Reflect on your calling. Jesus has chosen you to deliver His message and be the instrument of restoration and redemption. Open your mouth, be filled with My love, call the world to repentance, and share the Good News. Let the river of My Spirit rush forth from your life and wipe Satan and his works from the face of the earth.

My Prayer

Father, I give You thanks and glory for choosing me to have faith in Jesus. I know I was never worthy of the gift of Your Spirit who lives within me. Even after professing Jesus as my Savior, I still faltered, allowing my heart to turn away, my mind to be filled with distortions of truth. Like Adam and Eve in the Garden, I have turned my ears away many times from Your voice and listened to another. The news media, internet, teachers, coworkers, friends, and neighbors all vied for my attention. I consumed the forbidden and found it sweet. Greed, lust, the need for wealth and position—they were intoxicating and exhilarating. I thought I had found freedom, but I readily gave myself over to enslavement. My revulsion for worship with the community of believers grew, and I ended fellowship. I felt self-satisfied, powerful in my belief that I alone was the author of truth.

"My people have committed two sins: They have forsaken me, the spring of living water, and have dug their own cisterns, broken cisterns that cannot hold water" (Jeremiah 2:13).

I was neither hot nor cold, but lukewarm—indifferent to faith and religion. The way of Jesus meant nothing to me. I dismissed the Spirit and walked alone. I was the broken cistern.

But then the floodgates opened, and Your Spirit swept the darkness from my mind. The mask of evil fell away, and

I saw the face of Satan at my side. Lies. I had told myself lies. I awakened from my sleep and realized, Father, that nothing has value or meaning apart from You. Your voice alone is true. You have the words of eternal life. You are God, and there is no other. Jesus is Your Son, and Your love for us is the Spirit!

Restore me to fellowship, Father. Make me part of Your body again. Allow the rushing wind and blazing flame of the Spirit of Jesus to sweep me into Your arms. You are the comfort of Your people, Lord. Open the floodgates and let the living waters of Your Spirit wash away my offenses, heal my blindness, part my lips, clear my thoughts, and set my heart ablaze with love for You.

Living water, Holy Spirit, convict me in my faith. Strengthen my resolve to pray each day and keep my mind fixed on Jesus. Still my anxious mind and tormented thoughts. Breathe peace on my heart. Make me faithful to the commandments so that Your Spirit may find a true home within me. Prune away the habits and people that inhibit the life of the Spirit, Father. Command the living water to bear the fruits of kindness, patience, humility, fortitude, courage, faith, and fidelity. Let Your joy be complete within me. Draw near and remind me that the world hated You first. My home is not here. Living water, Spirit of God, prove the world wrong about sin, righteousness, and judgment. Guide me to all truth. Make known to me the will of the Father and lead me in the Way. "Don't you know that you yourselves are God's temple and that God's Spirit dwells in your midst?" (1 Corinthians 3:16).

Jesus, You have overcome the world, so shepherd me in Your steps. Your sacrifice on the cross paid my way and brought forgiveness for my sins. Walk with me now in this final journey. Sanctify the truth within my heart and use my mouth like a spring to bring the living water to the world. Shape and use me in such a way that I may give You glory. The spring opens, and the water of life flows. You gave me faith, so let me clear a way for the living water to cleanse the earth. Jesus, You are the answer to our deepest universal needs. Quench our thirst for meaning, fill the emptiness, satisfy our hunger. You are the rock of my salvation.

All human life is sustained by water, and all spiritual life begins with the Spirit. "Whoever believes in me, as Scripture has said, rivers of living water will flow from within them" (John 7:38). You have called me, Jesus, to the door, the spring, the gateway to the Kingdom. Your words fracture the physical world and reveal an opening to the spiritual. "Here I am! I stand at the door and knock. If anyone hears my voice and opens the door, I will come in and eat with that person, and they with me" (Revelation 3:20). I have a vision of the Jerusalem temple. I see water gushing forth from every crevice on the temple floor. The water pours through the doors, expands, and forms rivers stretching out to cover the earth. "Don't you know that you yourselves are God's temple and that God's Spirit wells in your midst?" (1 Corinthians 3:16). Jesus, I am Your temple, and You are the spring of living water welling up from within my heart. Wash away from my life all that I have spoiled. "Create in me a pure heart, O God, and renew a steadfast spirit within me. Restore to me the joy of your salvation and grant me a willing spirit, to sustain me" (Psalm 51:10,12). Use me according to Your design that I might fulfill the purpose for which You made me. Spirit of the living God, come forth and make me one with You.

Spoken in the Spirit through Jesus, the Son, to the Father. Amen.

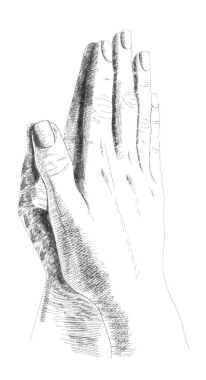

CHAPTER 35

GOD WILL PROVIDE A WAY

God is speaking to you. Listen!

My child, I want to speak to you who have reached the end of your resources and feel utterly helpless. There are times when the walls seem to close in, and the path ahead is shrouded in darkness. In these moments of trial, you may feel trapped, with no clear escape in sight. The weight of financial burdens, health issues, career challenges, family responsibilities, and the relentless passage of time—these are just a few of the chains that may bind you. As the walls of despair close in, your mind races, seeking a way out. How can you break free from this confinement? What options lie beyond these walls? The quest for liberation can be exhausting, the burden overwhelming. Yet, in these moments of uncertainty, when hope fades and despair looms large, remember that you are not alone.

Reflect on the example of My Son, Jesus. He faced countless challenges and could have given up many times, but He turned to Me and entrusted Himself to My care. Jesus never faced a day without first coming face to face with Me. Follow His example. Jesus made time to pray, to reach out and take My hand. In the footsteps of My Son, Jesus, who sought My divine guidance at every turn, fix your gaze upon Me and My strength. "Look to the LORD and his strength; seek his face always" (1 Chronicles 16:11).

Elijah, the prophet, looked to Me when life was overwhelming. Even as his world crumbled, Elijah did everything I asked of him. Yet he eventually fell prostrate to the ground, his face in the earth, praying for death. The prophet lacked the energy to take another step, let alone face the many problems that overwhelmed him. Perhaps you find yourself where Elijah was—in the wilderness, defeated, overpowered by darkness, without the strength to rise and face another day. Reflect on the chains that bind you—finances, health issues, family troubles, aging parents, betrayal. There is no limit to the burdens you may carry.

When the shadows of confinement loom large, rather than toiling in vain, surrender your spirit into My hands. Without Me, you will not succeed. Turn to Me, the light, lest the darkness consume you. Focus solely on what is going wrong, and your problems will grow larger. Your life is like a ship you were never meant to navigate alone. I sent My Spirit to dwell within you for a reason. My Spirit resides within you, a beacon to guide your steps and unveil My grand design. My Spirit serves as the stars in the night and the wind that propels by day.

Lift your head and look around you. Countless are the stories of believers who have witnessed My miraculous hand paving the way through the darkest valleys. "Forget the former things; do not dwell on the past. See, I am doing a new thing! Now it springs up; do you not perceive it? I am making a way in the wilderness and streams in the wasteland" (Isaiah 43:18-19). There are many true stories that witness to My provision in need—young couples who want a family, an adult child who escaped the cycle of addiction, the healing of a broken body or spirit. I provide loving spouses, resolve medical issues, help with employment, and strengthen faith. Reflect on these miracles and know that I am the Way-Maker.

Like the resilient apostle Paul, who never faltered in his faith, trust that I will always carve a path ahead. "We are hard-pressed on every side, but not crushed; perplexed, but not in despair; persecuted, but not abandoned; struck down, but not destroyed. . . So we fix our eyes not on what is seen, but on what is unseen, since what is seen is temporary, but what is unseen is eternal" (2 Corinthians 4:8-9,18). Live in this world with your focus on Me, and I will show you the way forward. If necessary, I will pick you up and carry you. Never accept defeat as an option. There were many times when I had to carry Paul, but together we always found a way. I am the Way-Maker.

Recall the scene when Paul and Silas were imprisoned. Were they lying face down in despair? No! They were praying and singing hymns. Prisons in those times were horrific places of unspeakable suffering and death. Yet Paul and Silas were not consumed with worry about tomorrow. They saw beyond the darkness, the cries of fellow prisoners, the stench, and the stale air. They looked into the face of Jesus, the light. Though physically imprisoned, they were free and celebrated their blessings. They did not give themselves over to fear but occupied themselves with giving glory and praise to Me! They surrendered their situation to Me and prayed, "Thy will be done." An earthquake followed. The prison doors flew open, and their chains fell off. Just as I made a way for them to leave the prison, trust that I will make a way for you.

You are not alone. The battle to rise from despair is one that everyone must face. Life is not always easy, and the path forward is not always clear. Reflect on the words of the contemporary Christian song "Way Maker" by Leeland, based on Isaiah 43:1-15. The song speaks of My work, for I am the Way-Maker. Just as I made a way for Israel through the Red Sea, I continue to make a way for My children through physical and mental suffering, broken relationships, and shattered dreams. There is power in My name and it stands supreme over depression, cancer, addiction, and betrayal. My name is all-powerful. I am the Way-Maker!

In the face of adversity, let go of the need for explanations and trust in My divine plan. "Trust in the LORD with all your heart and lean not on your own understanding; in all your ways submit to him, and he will make your paths straight" (Proverbs 3:5-6). When you need a way forward, call upon the name of Jesus and invoke His divine presence. Jesus Himself said, "And surely I am with you always, to the very end of the age" (Matthew 28:20). Turn to Me through Jesus, My Son, and our Holy Spirit will be within you.

My Prayer

Jesus, I give You praise and glory for the gift of faith. Thank You.

You, Jesus, are the way, the truth, and the life. You are the way forward. With Your Spirit, Lord, I can rise up and find a way. You are the way out of addiction, bad habits, prison, broken relationships and temptation. So many situations may seem impossible until I turn to You. You are in control.

With You in control, an alcoholic buying groceries ends up buying only groceries instead of visiting a liquor store. With You in charge, someone surfing the internet successfully watches a podcast without straying to harmful sites. With You in my life, I am kinder, more compassionate, disciplined, and prayerful. With You, Holy Spirit, spouses preserve their faithfulness, forgive, support, and encourage each other. You help us find peace in the present and trust the future to Your providence. "No temptation has overtaken you except what is common to mankind. And God is faithful; he will not let you be tempted beyond what you can bear. But when you are tempted, he will also provide a way out so that you can endure it" (1 Corinthians 10:13).

You speak tenderly to my brokenness, Lord, and lift me up when I am overwhelmed with fear. "Have I not commanded you? Be strong and courageous. Do not be afraid; do not be discouraged, for the LORD your God will be with you wherever you go" (Joshua 1:9).

"I can do all this through him who gives me strength" (Philippians 4:13). You, Lord God, have set the boundaries of the oceans and raised mountains to the sky. You led Israel out of bondage into the Promised Land. You closed the mouths of lions for Daniel, rained manna from the sky for the hungry Israelites, and stepped into the fiery furnace with Shadrach, Meshach, and Abednego. You healed the lepers and raised the dead to life. You helped David defeat a giant and miraculously fed five thousand and their families with just a few pieces of fish and bread. You are the God of impossible situations, and I cannot be defeated unless it is Your will. You are the Way-Maker, Jesus. You are the Way. You are with me and in me. All glory to You. I proclaim Your name, Lord, for You do impossible things for Your sons and daughters.

You brought good from every bad experience for St. Paul, and so shall it be for me. Every setback serves as a reminder that I need to rely fully on You, Lord, and not on my own resources.

As Paul sought solace in the prayers of his brethren, I too seek the communion of believers, recognizing strength in unity. Together, as one body, we stand, each bearing unique gifts, united in faith. May my trials strengthen my bond with You and with Your people, Lord, for in unity lies strength. I often stand apart from the community of believers. I try to resolve my own problems instead of utilizing the prayer power of Your church. It is "our" Father in the prayer Jesus taught, not "my" Father. Help me to remember that some problems cannot be resolved without the fellowship of believers. Help me understand how much I need other Christians. You have given different gifts to each of us, drawing us together as one body. Jesus, You are the Way-Maker, and Your way calls me into communion.

Jesus, You don't owe me any explanations. " 'For my thoughts are not your thoughts, neither are your ways my ways,' declares the LORD. 'As the heavens are higher than the earth, so are My ways higher than your ways and my thoughts than your thoughts' " (Isaiah 55:8-9). I don't need to spend time pondering why bad things happen. They are part of everyone's journey. Help me remember this when bad things happen, and I feel there is no way forward. My task is simple—reach out to You, Lord, and stand as one within Your body on earth.

Jesus said, "In this world, you will have trouble. But take heart! I have overcome the world" (John 16:33). Yes, Jesus, I find myself overwhelmed many times, but You are the way. You are victorious. You have overcome the world. "Come near to God, and he will come near to you" (James 4:8a). Like Job, I declare Your glory, Lord, and I know that You can do all things. No purpose of Yours can be thwarted (Job 42:2). Mary knew at the Annunciation that "For no word from God will ever fail" (Luke 1:37). Let every setback or defeat strengthen my communion with You, Lord, and with Your people. Help me, Lord, to trust, especially when I don't understand.

Spoken in the Spirit through Jesus, the Son, to the Father. Amen.

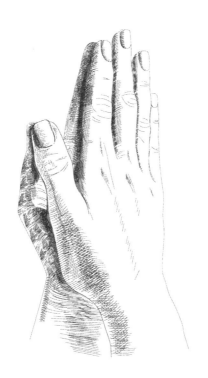

CHAPTER 36

ANGELS WATCH OVER YOU

God is speaking to you. Listen!

My child, be still and know that I am with you. Listen closely, for I speak to you of the angels who watch over you, protecting you in ways unseen. Jesus Himself said, "Do not despise these little ones, for I tell you that their angels in heaven always see the face of my Father in heaven" (Matthew 18:10). My love for you is so vast that it extends beyond your world, reaching even to the angels and holy ones who stand before My throne. How incredible is it that beings without physical form choose to love, care for, and guide you? Though they lack bodies, angels are not devoid of emotion (James 2:19), intelligence (2 Corinthians 11:3), or the free will to serve (2 Timothy 2:26). Consider the depth of their devotion, and let it fill your heart with awe.

Throughout the sacred Scriptures, angels have appeared in human history, offering guidance, assistance, and direction. King David, a man after My own heart, sang of their protective presence: "For he will command his angels concerning you to guard you in all your ways; they will lift you up in their hands so that you will not strike your foot against a stone" (Psalm 91:11-12). Acknowledge the breath of My love that sends guardians to your side. When the apostle Peter was imprisoned, the prayers of the faithful ascended to Me, and angels responded. They are also aware of your needs, and their prayers mingle with yours, rising before the throne of the Lamb. Remember the moment when I sent an angel to Peter, striking him on the side, causing his chains to fall away, and leading him to freedom. I send angels to you, even now, in your own moments of need.

Angels are not only protectors but worshipers. Thousands upon thousands gather joyfully in the heavenly Jerusalem, praising Me with unending devotion (Hebrews 12:22). In a vision, John the Evangelist saw a multitude of angels surrounding My throne, declaring, "Worthy is the Lamb who was slain to receive power and wealth and wisdom and strength and honor and glory and praise!" (Revelation 5:12). Their worship is pure, their devotion unwavering. Consider the incense rising from the altar in John's vision—a symbol of prayer, representing the prayers of angels intertwined with those of My people (Revelation 8:4). Let the unity of heaven and earth, inspire you to deepen your own prayers. How would angels know your prayers if they were not intimately involved in your life? Ponder this mystery and find comfort in their presence.

Angels hold a deep affection for humanity, and specific individuals are dear to them. In the second century before Christ, a book was written by a man named Tobit, reflecting elements of Jewish faith. Tobit encountered a stranger named Raphael, who assisted him in various ways. At the story's end, Raphael revealed his true identity: "I am Raphael, one of the seven angels who who stand ready and enter before the glory of the Lord" (Tobit 12:15 NRSV).[3] "I will now declare the whole truth to you and will conceal nothing from you. Already I have declared it you when I said, 'It is good to conceal the secret of a king, but to reveal with due honor the works of God.' So now when you and Sarah prayed, it was I who brought and read the record of your prayer before the glory of the Lord, and likewise whenever you would bury the dead" (Tobit 12:12 NRSV) This ancient document should give you some insight and understanding of John's vision in Revelation where the angels and saints are offering prayers before God's throne? Christ is the sole intercessor, yet seeking prayers from one another and from angels fosters unity and strengthens the bonds of love among you. It delights Me when you share not only your blessings but also your needs with one another and with those in heaven both the angels and the holy ones. My desire is that you all become one, this is communion. Never forget that no one comes to Me except through Christ.

I allow angels to communicate with you through dreams, visions, and personal encounters. Think of Joseph, who was warned by an angel in a dream about King Herod's plans. Gabriel appeared to Mary to announce the birth of My Son. An angel instructed Joseph to take Mary as his wife and later to flee from Herod's wrath. I have sent angels to you personally many times. Have you ever paused to wonder about the unseen forces guiding you? Consider the presence of angels in your life to be nothing more than a manifestation of My unwavering love and protection.

---

3   (NRSV) New Revised Standard Version Bible, National
     Council of Churches of Christ in the U.S.A. 1989. (Internet:
     www.BibleStudyTools.com)

My Prayer

Jesus, my King, Your creation is vast and filled with wonders beyond my understanding. You are an awe-inspiring and magnificent God, and I am forever grateful for Your mercy and love.

I humbly acknowledge that You have created angels to watch over and protect me. Your design for creation is so intricate that it allows angels to engage with Your children, guiding and shielding us in ways, ways we may never fully comprehend. I marvel at the thought that angels have intervened in my life, no doubt often without any awareness on my part. Was it an angel who prompted me to double-check the side-view mirror before changing lanes? Was it an angel who kept me safe at home on the night of an accident? Was it an angel who carried me through a moment of despair when I felt like giving up? I am deeply moved by the knowledge that angels have always been at my side, even now, joining me in prayer to the Lamb.

Lord, grant me the discernment to heed the voices of the angels You send to guard over me. Your Spirit guides me in distinguishing which voices to listen to and follow. I understand that not all angels are benevolent; therefore, I implore You to grant me clarity and understanding so that I may discern the nature of the voices that speak to my heart. Help me to cultivate the humility to surrender my plans and my will to Your guidance. Through Your Holy Spirit, empower me to stand firm in Your truth and follow the example of Jesus.

Just as angels accompanied Jesus throughout His life—from the annunciation of His birth, through His childhood, to His death and resurrection—I wholeheartedly welcome the company and friendship of Your angels on my own journey. May they remind me when it is time to pray, and may they join me in dedicating my body, mind, and spirit to You. May the angels unite their prayers with mine, like incense rising before the Lamb, and may You graciously listen and respond according to Your holy will. May Your holy angels shield me from evil, guide my steps, inspire my words, and fill my heart with love for You and for my sisters and brothers.

Spoken in the Spirit through Jesus the Son to the Father. Amen.

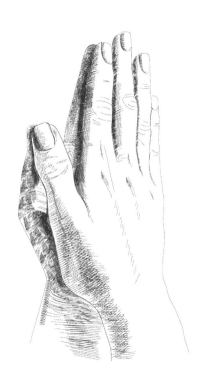

CHAPTER 37

MY PEACE I GIVE TO YOU

God is speaking to you. Listen!

Jesus said, "Peace I leave with you; My peace I give you. I do not give to you as the world gives. Do not let your hearts be troubled and do not be afraid" (John 14:27). The world seeks peace by removing conflict, striving for an absence of turmoil, animosity, and war. But the peace I offer is not merely the absence of hardship—it is a presence, a profound restoration of wholeness that transcends understanding. This peace, born of the Holy Spirit, fills you with a tranquility that the world cannot offer. It is a peace that endures, independent of the chaos that may surround you, rooted in the communion you share with Me.

I am peace itself, a perfect communion of three persons in one. Your union with Me through the indwelling of My Spirit draws you into the fullness of what I envisioned for you at the dawn of creation. Through this communion, you enter a journey toward wholeness. Peace and communion are intertwined, inseparable experiences. "But now in Christ Jesus, you who once were far away have been brought near by the blood of Christ. For he himself is our peace" (Ephesians 2:13-14). In My love, I draw you into Myself through Jesus. Remember the words of Christ: "No one comes to the Father except through me" (John 14:6). Let these truths guide you, as you allow My peace to sanctify every part of your being—spirit, soul, and body—keeping you blameless until the coming of our Lord Jesus Christ (1 Thessalonians 5:23).

The peace of Christ is a state of being, a gift that cannot be earned, claimed, or demanded. As the Spirit of Christ grows within you, so too does the tranquility, harmony, and communion that reflect My very nature. "On that day you will realize that I am in my Father, and you are in me, and I am in you" (John 14:20). This profound unity is a oneness that transcends all earthly understanding and circumstances.

This peace is not dependent on what happens around you—it is not shaken by the storms of life. Consider the Apostle Paul, who spoke of a peace that surpasses all understanding (Philippians 4:7). Even when the world around you is in turmoil, the peace of Christ remains steadfast, unbroken. The early Christian martyrs, who sang hymns of praise even as they faced death, knew My peace. Their peace was not found in their circumstances but in their deep spiritual connection with Me. Let this inspire you to seek that same peace, not in the world, but in Me through the indwelling of the Spirit.

Jesus is the way to this peace. "Come near to God, and he will come near to you. Wash your hands, you sinners, and purify your hearts, you double-minded" (James 4:8). Jesus, the Lamb who takes away your sins, restores your relationship with Me, your Creator. The power of Jesus's sacrifice makes this possible. This peace necessitates that you trust Me enough to surrender your life into My care through Jesus. When you place Me on the throne of your heart, My voice alone should guide your actions and decisions. I call you out of the world's turmoil and into a timeless communion with Me, where true peace resides.

Every loving relationship is both a gift and a journey. Marriage, for example, is a sacred bond that requires vigilance to maintain communion. Just as metals are refined through fire, so too is your communion in marriage is deepened and strengthened as you navigate life's challenges together. The same is true of your relationship with Me for our ever-evolving communion is shaped by your daily choices. You must be vigilant to protect and nurture all your relationships founded in love.

One key to preserving your communion with Me is to grow in knowledge. To know Me is to love Me, for I am love itself. Do not all loving relationships deepen through knowledge, leading to greater peace and unity. It is through the Spirit—pure, holy, and spiritual—that our bond is formed, a bond that nothing should separate, break, or divide (Romans 8:38-39). Let this truth inspire you to seek a deeper understanding of Me, knowing that this knowledge will strengthen our communion.

St. Peter warns against complacency in your peace. He encourages you to "add to your faith goodness; and to goodness, knowledge; and to knowledge, self-control; and to self-control, perseverance; and to perseverance, godliness; and to godliness, mutual affection; and to mutual affection, love" (2 Peter 1:5-7). The peace born of communion with Me needs your constant vigilance. There is no loving communion, painstakingly built over a lifetime, that cannot be shattered in a moment of recklessness. Your relationship with Me will be tested by the forces of the world. Embrace your test and turn your trials into an opportunity to deepen our bond.

Vigilance in preserving in peace means being aware of how your attitudes and choices can threaten our communion. Reflect on the need to choose peace over worry and fear. Trusting in Me does not mean that I will grant every desire, but that I will provide what you truly need. Your trust in Me will not prevent challenges so do not be complacent with our relationship. Bad things will happen, even to those with the strongest faith, but persevere and trust in My benevolence. Faith means believing in My goodness, even when circumstances suggest otherwise. Remember this when things go badly and surrender your burdens to My care (1 Peter 5:7).

Imagine a mother bird stretching out her wings, providing warmth and protection to her young. This image beautifully reflects our communion. When you feel threatened or weary, call this image to mind. Ask Me for your daily bread, for deliverance from evil, and for the grace to forgive. The peace of Christ does not eliminate the powers of darkness but provides shelter in the storm. Make Me your refuge, dwell beneath My wings. Reflect on the words of the Psalmist: "If you say 'The LORD is my refuge' and you make the Most High your dwelling, no harm will overtake you, no disaster will come near your tent. For He will command his angels concerning you to guard you in all your ways; they will lift you in their hands so that you will not strike your foot against a stone" (Psalm 91:9-12).

My Prayer

Lord Jesus, I am grateful that You spoke my name and called me to Yourself. Your gift of faith has given meaning and purpose to my life. I know and believe I was made for Your pleasure. It is only with You as my guide and shepherd that I will grow in communion with You and ultimately become the person You originally envisioned at my creation.

I admire You, Jesus, for Your unwavering trust in the Father, even as the world collapsed around You on Good

Friday. You surrendered completely to God's will and placed Yourself beneath the Father's wings. You and the Father are one. You are perfect peace. At Your birth, the angels proclaimed the glory of God and prophesied peace on those You favor (Luke 2:14). I ask You, Jesus, to look with favor upon me. I cannot earn Your love or forgiveness, for I am a mere creature. It is only by Your grace that I can hear Your voice and believe that the Father sent You. It is only through Your love that I open my heart to Your peace and surrender myself into Your care. Help me to rest in Your peace, Jesus, content to live one day at a time, trusting in Your friendship and guidance.

I am ashamed that despite my faith, I am often overcome with worry and anxiety. I allow the struggles of my brothers and sisters, the suffering I see in the world, and my own fears to rob me of peace. Despite Your caution, Lord, I allow fear to consume me. Reflecting on this, I realize that I may be fighting against deep-seated wounds from my past or a natural tendency toward worry. Lord, I beg You to make my faith in You real; break through the darkness of my doubts. Show me Your face. Lift me from the waters that threaten to pull me away from You. Let me feel Your comforting hand on my shoulder. Breathe on me, Jesus. Whisper Your words of comfort into my mind. Draw me into communion with You, and let Your peace fill every corner of my soul. Live within me, make me whole, and finish the work You have begun. I long for nothing more than to be in Your presence, to know Your peace, and to be shielded from all that seeks to take my eyes off You.

You are the center of my life, Jesus, so I pledge to continue to open Scripture and ask for Your Spirit to fill me, hold me, sustain me, strengthen me, and protect me. May my knowledge of You increase and dispel doubt. Fortify my love. I know the Scriptures are a door I need to walk through to become a firsthand witness to Your words and actions. Help me to be more disciplined and attentive in my study of Your Word. Each story offers the opportunity to sit at Your feet, Jesus, to follow You on Your earthly journey, and to share in Your mission. Help me feed on Your Word, Lord, and let it work in my flesh that I might become the best version of myself.

Thank You for allowing me a place on the mountain as You fed the crowd with fish and bread. Thank You for the privilege of standing in Jerusalem to greet You at Your triumphal entry. It is a gift to stand with John and Mary beneath the cross. I am blessed to see Mary of Magdala greet You outside the empty tomb. Communion with You, Lord, is no longer just an intellectual exercise of affirmation but a matter of mind, body, and spirit wherein I enter Your story, and You become my story.

Jesus, save me and save the world! I know You must be saddened by the horrific crimes against Your love perpetrated every day in countries around the world. Intervene in history and end the chaos that pits one person against another. Enlighten and empower people everywhere to reach out to You and bring Your Spirit into daily life. Let Your kingdom come on earth as it is in heaven. You, Lord Jesus, are "Wonderful Counselor, Mighty God, Everlasting Father, Prince of Peace" (Isaiah 9:6).

I pray, Jesus, that the communion You have shared with me may be shared with others. Please gift the people I love and all the world with faith in Your name. Lift their vision beyond the problems and tasks of this world to see in Your eyes the truth revealed in all its fullness. As my communion with You continues to mature, Lord, send Your Spirit to connect with and draw others into Your divine life.

Together, may the day come when we all stand before Your throne with all the holy ones and give You glory and praise.

Spoken in the Spirit through Jesus, the Son, to the Father. Amen.

If you enjoyed these prayers and think others might benefit from them, please consider reviewing the book on Amazon.

Author's mailing address is:
PO Box 7. Clifford, PA 18413-007.

Author's email: symeon.7.theologian@gmail.com

Made in United States
Orlando, FL
06 December 2024